THE CUBICLE DIARIES

(A Reality Novel)

By

JADEN ARMANI
St. Petersburg, Florida, USA

This book is a work of fiction. Names, characters, places and incidents are the product of the author's imagination or are used fictitiously. Any resemblance to actual events, locales or persons, living or dead, is coincidental.

Marriage is a wonderful institution.

Many of us enter into it with aspirations and expectations of green pastures and oceans of roses.

Your bride is the most beautiful woman in the world, and for women, the groom the most handsome.

The majority of us do not realize what effect time has on the young couple.

The grass may not be green all the time, keep in mind we do have changes of seasons.

The oceans of roses may not bloom as they should, and winters can be extremely long.

Love should be able to withstand any season, and soften any thorns that might arise.

Your spouse should always be the majority of all your thoughts, and you should love him or her endlessly.

The Cubicle's Synopsis

Curtis and Grace had the perfect marriage, or so it seemed. Both were successful and had learned to balance their professional careers with their personal lives. Things could not be any better—that is, until Curtis had to alter his career to help with the growing demands of his family. Although his new job would be a perfect fit for his home life, it would throw him into an arena in which he didn't understand the rules. Corporate America has completely changed in the past twenty years; there are more women and men working side by side in offices all over the country. In the same way that children tend to know their babysitters better than their parents, spouses are becoming better acquainted to people with whom they are spending a majority of their day. When Curtis met Janice, he had never looked twice at another woman and had no intention of leaving his home. Yet fate sometime steps in the way of our plans and deals blows from which we never recover. She would be the chosen one. He realized that she hated men just enough to bring his perfect world crumbling down around him like the towers on 911. Even though Janice was the catalyst that ended his marriage, they continued the charade of the relationship until Janice's insecurities put an end to the already doomed courtship. Then she would drop out of his life with a bang. While still reeling from his separation from Grace, he ended up finding solace in the arms of a married woman. Curtis became fond of Anne knowing that she was having marital issues and was vulnerable to his advances, and all at the same time, he knew that was the reason for his predicament. Curtis had to do something to break things off when their relationship became sexual. He started reaching out to different women at work and talking to anyone willing to listen. Curtis would continue this path until he met up with a woman with a narcissist personality; an unexpected event took hold of him and shook him to his core. After this encounter, Curtis exiled himself from all he knew. He became a stranger within himself. His life went spiraling down, and he had no ambition to regain control. His fate now lay in the hands of this cruel and heartless world. How could it all end like this?

1

The Beginning of the End

He had squandered over $70,000 in less than two months and realized that he may never see the light of day again. He had no desire to leave his house and had accepted the fact that he would soon perish there. The smell of rotten food finally started to penetrate the door of the refrigerator. The power had been off for over a month, and the dishes had not been cleaned in over two. The food-encrusted plates were the last sign of a time that now seemed so far away. Roaches were overrunning the house, but Curtis seemed oblivious to it all. It had been over a month since he walked outside and even longer since he had a changed his clothes. The only thing he lived for was one more hit of that glass bitch that never failed him. He was spiraling down, with no way to recover. He had alienated everyone he knew.

Every now and then, the neighbor's cat would shimmy his way through the screen in the window and come down to visit Curtis until the cat food he kept around was gone.

"Well, Mister Cat, this is the last of it," Curtis said to the cat, refer-
ring to the food that was left in the apartment when he moved in. "I
guess you are going to leave me like every other pussy that has entered
my life."

The cat looked up and meowed as if to say, "What do you expect?
You are out of food."

As the cat ate the last nibble of the Meow Mix, Curtis threw the
crumpled up empty bag at the kitten, "Get the hell out of here. I'm tired
of feeding you anyway." The cat quickly dashed off but didn't leave
the room. "Why are you still here?" he said, as he raised his head and
looked at the cat. "Didn't I tell you I was out of food?"

The cat purred and started, and then made his way back to Curtis. The
cat had come around every day for the past two months as though a witness for Curtis's demise. For Curtis, in his present state, was a shadow of
the man he had been only months ago. His one time well-tuned body was
now frail, his unshaven face lifeless. As he ran his fingers through the
nappy hair that had grown on his face, he apologized to the cat for being
cruel. As if he understood, the cat rubbed his body up against Curtis's
leg. He seemed not to mind that Curtis reeked of urine. Although Curtis
would try to make it to the toilet, which was already overflowing with
feces, most of the time he'd find he had fallen short and was already pissing in his clothes. Other than the cat, the only visitor he would get was
the neighborhood drug boy who didn't give a damn about the person he
sold to, as long as the money was good. Every three days or so he would
appear at the door, and Curtis would put $1,000 through the mail slot. In
return, he would get a substantial amount of crack.

Curtis had withdrawn over $50,000 out of his account and exiled
himself from the rest of the world. He had rented a small one-bedroom
apartment in his old neighborhood and cut himself off from everyone,
even his children. He was tired of giving his all to everyone he knew and
getting nothing in return. Everyone he knew only wanted what he or she
could get from him. The only people he would miss were his kids. On his
last trip to the bank, he opened an account for both of them and placed
over $80,000 in each account. He knew that he was possibly on a one-
way trip and wanted to be sure that he left something for his kids.

Curtis couldn't believe that life would ever get the best of him.
He had always been on top of his game. Before he married Grace,

Curtis always excelled in money matters. He was the first kid in the neighborhood to get a car. Although he played football with the rest of his friends, Curtis always had a job. By the time he graduated, he had saved enough money for a down payment on his first house. He tried university life only to realize that he could make more money than most of the people who would graduate from college. He met Grace in his brief time at the school in their hometown. They married and not too long after had their first kid. Curtis quit school and put all of his efforts into his work. By the time he was twenty-five, Curtis had been promoted to management. He had embarked on the good life. He had saved a great deal of money so that before he reached thirty, he was able to buy the house of his dreams. By that time, his second kid had been born, and he seemed to be truly living the American dream. He always made the right decisions, and even when he made poor choices, things always seemed to work out, as though he were blessed with an angel on his shoulder.

Curtis had always been a generous person and would always help anyone in need. It did not occur in one moment, but finally he had gotten to a point where he was disgusted with the human race. He could not believe how deceptive people could be. No matter how many times he tried to put his trust in someone, it would turn out to be another person with an angle. Although most people he knew percieved, him to be the happy go lucky person that outwardly we all are Curtis inwardly had grown tired of most people within his circle.

"You know what, Mister Cat, you are the only creature of God that actually seems to care, but what in the hell is your angle?" Curtis started to get angry again. "Why can't you just get the hell out of here and leave me alone? What are you waiting on, my carcass to nibble on when I die?"

Reality began setting in after Curtis threw the dirty, empty bag, and it bounced off the cat's behind. He realized that he might not see his children again. He reached for a pen and started to write on the inside of the bag he had just thrown at the cat.

To my children Leigh and Junior,

You know that I have always loved you with all my heart. I have always said that life was hard, and if you weren't smart enough to understand it, that it would consume you. I also said that life was unfair and warned you not to take anything or anyone for granted. Life has its up and downs, but if you continue to strive for the stars, remember, I always told you, you wouldn't come up short. Continue to live in the way I taught you and don't let anyone get the best of you. Find someone that truly loves you and don't settle for anything less than the best. I think I have two of the world's greatest kids and don't you ever forget that. I want you to know that I have lived the best life that I could have imagined, and it was due to you two. Now that you two are adults and have great futures ahead of you, I know that I have done my job. I am now calling it quits. I have had enough fun to last two lifetimes, and there is nothing left for me to do here. Tell your mother that I apologize for screwing up her life. I really didn't mean for her to be a casualty in all of this, and I never stopped loving her. Please take care of your grandmother for me. I had always told her that I would be there for her no matter what, and I need for you to keep that promise for me. Always remember you two are the most important people in my life, and I just hope one day you can understand why I had to leave you. I have lived my life for you, and now I need to end mine for me.

Love your dad, forever.

Curtis dropped the pen and placed the paper on the table next to his bed. He had given the dope boy over $3,000 on his last visit. There was enough crack on the table to last him a month. Curtis pulled out the bottle of Grey Goose he had been hiding in his night-stand for a special occasion, poured a full glass, and didn't bother to chase it down. He then piled all the rocks he could into the bowl of his glass pipe and started smoking it until there was nothing left. As he inhaled the last bowl, he was already drenched in sweat, and his heartbeat accelerated to Mars or some such planet. He bent over in his bed, and the sweat dripped from his brow. He thought, the only other bitch that made him sweat like that was Demetria. He laughed to himself, turned up the glass of vodka, and drank it. As he lowered the glass, his body started to go into convulsions. The lack of food in his system was breaking him down. The vodka went straight to his stomach, and he had the most painful burning in his abdomen. The glass in his hand crashed to the floor and pieces of glass scattered across the room, and his body started to tremble as he was beginning to go into shock. A few minutes went by, and he felt his life start to slip away. Everything got extremely calm. All he could think about was the day he was playing basketball in the driveway with his son. They used to have so much fun, and at the time, he thought those days would never end. As Curtis lay there in his bed, barely clinging on to life, he had a flashback of the events that lead him to this excruciating conclusion.

2
First Day

As Curtis sat in the human resources office, he was overwhelmed with the anxiety of starting a new job. It wasn't only a new job; it was also a total career change. He had worked in the home improvement field all of his adult life, and now that he had reached forty, he was about to give up his blue-collar job for a white-collar profession. What in the hell was he thinking?

When he and Grace decided that he would try to find a job that would be a little more family friendly, Curtis said that he would only leave his industry if he could find a job paying the same salary and benefits. Curtis didn't think he would find a job that would pay close to what he was making. He had an associate's degree, but knew that office jobs didn't pay much. Hell, he was making almost six figures, but he understood that being away from home so much would wear down his family and begin to adversely affect their children. Leigh was now seven, and Junior ten. Both were active in extracurricular activities. Grace's first year dealing with the preparations of taking them to and from practices alongside cooking and cleaning the house was what really brought on the idea of Curtis quitting his job. She wanted him there to help with the kids and not just every other weekend. The more he tried to look the other way, the more she pushed him to be actively involved.

Anyway, he had known this day would come. But while the best place for him was home, he also knew that his salary was the reason his family never wanted for anything, and he was doing something he really enjoyed. Moreover, that was rare for people, for most of his friends anyway. So after looking for a job for about three months, Curtis had found nothing that would replace what he would have been losing. One day Grace came home and told him that a coworker of hers had informed her of a company offering a position similar to what he was doing, but as a desk job. She said that her friend's husband was a manager there, and he would give Curtis a good recommendation.

So he decided to call to see what this position entailed. It was a buying position for a home improvement store, and because he knew the industry from the other side, it would be a perfect fit. The salary was a little less than what he was making; however, the incentives would make up for the variance. They also had a retirement plan that was superior to the one that he currently had. He really didn't want to work inside all the time, but he realized he would have to make a sacrifice somewhere. That's what marriage was all about, right? Curtis applied for the job and was hired on the spot. Either the husband of his wife's friend had a lot of influence, or they were impressed with his resume. He was sure it was the recommendation, but he wasn't about to ask questions. Curtis would find out more and more that in the corporate arena, it's mostly who you know.

Curtis arrived a few minutes early on his first day, and after about thirty minutes, he found himself following his new supervisor to his new desk. She apologized for being late when she'd finally appeared. He would also have to get used to having a woman boss. Not that he was chauvinistic, but there were no women to work with in his previous job. Before today, he had met with her on two other occasions, both times, she had worn a pantsuit, and he didn't pay much attention to her. When she approached Curtis this time, his attention immediately went to her legs. She had the most perfect legs he had seen on a woman. Her toes were freshly manicured with a toe ring on the middle toe. She was wearing a free flowing skirt that hugged her thighs and behind. And although she was a white woman, she had enough ass to turn his head. She also wore a low-cut blouse that accented the boob job she had no doubt received. This woman had to be in her midforties, but her body could easily compete with any twenty-year-old he knew. There was no way that this woman didn't hit the gym at least three times a week.

In the ten years he had worked on his other job he had never had direct contact with a person of this caliber. The women in the construction field wore jeans and a hard hat. The most excitement came during the rainy seasons. The guys would sometimes get a good wet T-shirt contest. Although Curtis didn't really like working indoors, this wasn't going to be all that bad if this was a preview of what was to come. But maybe this was just an isolated event. How could there be more women like this in the building?

After they left the human resources office, she took Curtis on a tour of the most frequently visited places. The first was the cafeteria. It was equipped with televisions and coffee machines where people were gathered. Since it was between lunch and breakfast, there were only a few people waiting on the coffee to finish brewing. They then left and proceeded through another department that seemed a haven for women. They were on an open floor plan with a couple hundred offices. There were women of all shapes, sizes, and color. The walls on the office were low, and as Curtis walked by, he could see heads raise and lower, as if all of these women were gophers on a golf course. A few men were working also, but there were so many women, the men were hardly noticeable. Curtis couldn't believe the number of women working in the area. As he passed, he tried not to look at anyone for an extended length of time. Just passed by and glanced. He would periodically wave at someone if it were applicable.

Delores informed him that this was the customer service department; this explained a few things immediately. Curtis was used to having his own office with a door and a clock on the wall. This was an entirely different atmosphere than he was accustomed to. There was no privacy, and if you sneezed, two or three people would say, "bless you." Everyone had headsets on and seemed to be busy. He knew this must be for the entry-level employees because a majority of those working appeared to be college age. These people were the backbone of the company and most likely were paid the least. This company was one of the largest in its industry with over a million customers in its base, and these entry-level employees talked to those customers on a daily basis. Although they were probably the lowest paid, they had to work the hardest.

As they passed through, he felt as though he was walking down a runway because everyone was looking. Most women made it obvious that they were looking. As they turned the corner and entered another department, it was more of the same. If Delores hadn't told him this was a different department, he wouldn't have known. It was a sea of women with a male thrown in every now and then. After walking for what seemed to be ten minutes, they finally got to the area where he would be working. The only thing he could see were walls of the same type in the previous area except these were a lot higher. The only way to see someone was to actually go past his or her office and look in.

As they approached his office, she introduced him to the employees that he would be working directly with. This area was a far cry from the ladies he had experienced on the way here. Even the woman to guy ratio was different here. There were eight guys and two women, one being the supervisor. This was what Curtis expected. As he reached his office, Delores explained that this was his cubicle and that IT would be by to help him set up his computer. Curtis asked her what she meant by cubicle, and she told him it was his office and that such types of offices were called cubicles. It made a lot of sense since they were all square.

For the rest of the day Curtis sat around and waited on the computer geeks to get him set up in the system.

On the way home from work, the only thing Curtis could think about was all the ass he had seen. He couldn't believe there were so many women in such a small geographical area. He knew that he was married to the most wonderful person in the world, and he loved her with all he had. Like any other relationship though, they had their problems from time to time. Still there was no other person he would rather be with. This job would truly put their relationship to the test. One woman in particular stood out in his mind the entire way home. The sound of a car horn stopped Curtis from daydreaming as the light changed to green; he laughed to himself as the driver behind him sped pass and put up his middle finger. He could not believe he didn't see the light change.

When he turned into his driveway, Curtis Jr. was playing basketball in the front yard, so he didn't pull all the way into the drive. He got out, loosened his tie, and dared him to a quick game of one on one. The basketball goal was always lower than average because his son liked to dunk the ball, so every chance Curtis got, he did his imitation of Dr. J. Before long he was soaking wet, his dress slacks were dirty and probably stained for good. He could always replace his pants, he thought, but the time that spent with his son was priceless. Before Curtis looked for Grace, he went into his daughter's room. He knew that she would be there talking on the phone or watching videos on her television. He snuck up behind her and hugged her, making sure she was just as sweaty as he was before he let her go. She hated when he did that, but her love for him would turn her frown upside down, and before you knew it, she was trying to find a way to get him back before he could run out of her room. Curtis noticed that she was going for her dresser.

"Okay, Dad, since you want to play, I got something for you," she said.

Before Curtis could dash out of the room, Leigh sprayed a heavy dose of her body spray on him, and he left her room smelling like a French princess. She knew her dad didn't like smelling like a woman. Curtis then made his way into the kitchen where Grace was cooking dinner. He walked up behind her, hugged her, and kissed the nape of her neck.

She recognized the scent of the body spray and said, "You've been messing with your daughter again, huh?"

Curtis just laughed, and as he asked her what was for dinner, Curtis slid his hand across Grace's ass and said, "I see what's for dessert."

As she started to tell him, he walked out to go into the bedroom to take a bath and get ready for dinner. The first thing he always did was find his newspaper. Grace yelled to him and said that it was already in the bathroom. She knew the first things he wanted were the three famous S's. Shit, shower, and shave. Curtis thanked her and said he would be out in a few minutes. She must have been waiting until she heard the toilet flush because the moment he finished and hopped in the shower, she too was getting in. This was something she never did, so Curtis asked what was going on.

"I figured I would give you your dessert early," she said as she reached down and grabbed Curtis's ass.

"So how did your first day at work go?" Grace asked.

"It was good, didn't do much, but I think it will be okay once I get used to being in one place all day. Are you okay? I'm surprised you are in here with me, especially at this time of day with the kids still up."

She said there was nothing going on, but Curtis thought between the sweat, the body spray, and the stroke on her ass, he had pressed a button that needed to be addressed, and she couldn't wait until tonight. He was always up to impromptu sex, but this was totally out of her character.

When they finished, Curtis went on to explain that he didn't think the job would be as bad as he had anticipated. For some reason he felt as if she knew exactly what he had experienced today. Hell, she had worked in a corporate environment all her life, and as Curtis thought about it, he became quite sure she had been one of those women he had seen today. Maybe this would explain the early escapade in the shower. She must have been thinking about it all day. She knew there was an abundance of females who worked there, and she was aware that most of them didn't give a fuck about someone's marriage. But she and Curtis had a special relationship, and she also knew that he would never screw that up. Maybe like him, deep down in her mind, she also knew that he wasn't perfect and their marriage hadn't been perfect either.

After about the first week, Curtis began to notice how Grace looked at him every morning as he dressed. He made every effort not to look his best, although he was very particular about his appearance. Everything had to be in the right place. Curtis had always been a good dresser; it would often make up for any imperfections he might have had. This was one of the things that attracted her to Curtis in the first place. Since he'd started this job though, Curtis's wardrobe had changed completely. He had purchased new clothes every pay period. Although he had plenty of dress clothes, he needed more casual attire, so he had to buy clothes more suited for the office. After two months of buying clothes, Grace finally asked him was he trying to impress someone at the office. He explained to her that most of his clothes were too dressy and that he had had to buy clothes more comfortable to work in. Although this was true, those clothes Curtis had purchased were also much more for flattering his body.

"You need to stop tripping, Grace. You know that I'm particular about how I dress, but I come home to you every day after work. And I'm going to continue to do that forever."

Grace listened for a minute and said, "I hope you don't ever have to eat those words."

Grace and Curtis met in high school but never dated. Curtis went off to the military for a couple of years and started college when he returned home. Grace had also enrolled there too. Curtis had always had a crush on her from the time he met her, but never had the nerve to ask her out. When they were reacquainted in college, his childhood shyness was far behind him and he decided one day to ask her out. Grace didn't respond the way he had hoped, and the disappointment reminded Curtis of why the childhood shyness exist. The reality of rejection was very hurtful to the young adult and most rather not experience it. However, Curtis wasn't going down without a fight. He asked Grace everyday and she refused everyday.

One day Curtis had taken a friend to pick up some photos that she had taken. While in the photo shop, he noticed that they had a large photo of Grace on the wall. It was the most beautiful image he had ever seen. He told the clerk that he wanted to buy it, because the picture was of his girlfriend and he wanted to surprise her. After a few minutes of persuasion, he purchased the photo. Curtis then went to the store and bought a extra large greeting card, place the picture in it and presented it to Grace the next time he saw her. When Grace opened the envelope, she was over-whelmed with emotion. Curtis had written; The most beautiful woman in the world on the inside of the card, and the smile he received was worth the cash he had spent on the picture. She finally agreed to go out with him and from that day on Curtis and Grace were inseperable and a perfect fit for each other. Curtis fell head over heels for Grace and asked her to marry him after several months of dating and the rest is history.

3

What's Going On

Months passed and things between Grace and Curtis started to get worse. Curtis was starting to get into the routine of the office employees. He started going to lunch with coworkers, hanging out with them on Fridays for happy hour, and even volunteered to work overtime. This irritated Grace more and more. Curtis didn't see anything wrong with it because he hadn't messed around with anyone. He was just doing what he thought was best based on his desire to become successful. Curtis was the type of guy to maximize any opportunity. Grace was content that she and Curtis had good jobs and were raising the kids without financial problems. Curtis was very ambitious and would do anything to get to the top of any company he worked for. She knew that, but this would eventually cause more arguments between them. And arguing, which had been new to their relationship at one time, went from once a month to once a week, sometimes more.

One night, after an especially intense round, Curtis had to get out of the house. He hated arguing while the kids were still up. He found himself driving down by the beach on one of the nicest nights of the year. The moon seemed uncommonly bright this night. It was as round as a basketball and appeared to be close enough to touch. He remembered taking walks along the coast with Grace before the kids came. Those were some of the happiest days of his life. He and Grace had even made love on the beach once or twice, probably conceived one of his children out here. Curtis kept going past the beach and decided to ride by Dwayne's house. His car wasn't there, so he kept going and ended up at the liquor store. Dwayne was always the voice of reason for Curtis, and without his advice tonight, Curtis would look for satisfaction in a bottle of Kettle One. After Curtis had a drink or two, he decided to go by and hang out with Galen. When he got to Galen's place, he stayed in the car for a while. Galen was not the friend to go to when he was having marital problems. Galen lived alone and was your typical bachelor. He never respected the institution of marriage and was convinced that everyone would eventually get divorced. He wasn't too far off base because all of the guys they had grown up with were divorced. Curtis was the exception, the only one still married. Curtis finally got out of the car and knocked on the door.

"What's up, Curtis, and why are you out drinking this time of night? You and Grace arguing, right?"

Curtis didn't want to answer; he knew that Galen would go straight for the jugular. "Yeah, we had a little misunderstanding, and I didn't want to argue with her because the kids were still up, so I just got out of there."

"Dwayne must not be home," Galen mused.

"Why do you say that?" Curtis asked.

"Because every time you and Grace are going through something, you always end up over there."

Curtis hadn't realized that Galen knew about the visits to Dwayne's. Obviously Dwayne had told him.

"That damn Dwayne," Curtis said.

"Hell, you shouldn't be surprised. We all are best friends. I don't know why you try and keep it from me anyway. I promise I will never tell you I told you so, but it's hard these days being married. There are too many single women," Galen went on to say. "And these women don't care about or respect a marriage. And as long as these married guys are knocking them off, this causes more and more trust issues amongst everyone. Hell, think about it, Curtis, if you were single and didn't want to get into a serious relationship, who would you date?" Curtis looked at Galen for a while without answering. "It would be someone already involved, right? Most women have screwed a married guy, so when they get married, they go into the marriage with trust issues," Galen continued.

The more Galen talked the more it started to make sense. He actually had a point. But Galen had always been the type to keep it real. Those who didn't want to hear would just distance themselves as Curtis had done in the past.

"What are you drinking?" Galen asked.

"I have a bottle of Kettle One," Curtis answered. "Are you drinking with me?"

Before Curtis could finish, Galen had already taken a glass from the cupboard. "Thought you would never ask," Galen said. "So what's going on with you and Grace?"

"She's accusing me of cheating on her again," Curtis answered.

"Well, the last time she did, she was correct, wasn't she?" Galen reminded him.

"Yeah, but that was years ago, and we got beyond that," Curtis answered.

"Let me tell you something, Curtis. You never get beyond that kind of thing. Hell, I'm not even married, but when I'm seeing someone and she finds out that I have cheated, it affects our relationship forever. It may not be obvious, but it never goes away. And it will resurface the moment your habits change. What you need to do is get you some since she is already accusing you of doing just that. It can't hurt! Hell, it may even put a little spice in your relationship," Galen said.

"Now you see why I don't come by here when Grace and I are going through something?" Curtis said. "You always end up talking the same way."

"You know, Curtis, you and Grace have been married for a long time, and sometimes it's good to just go out and meet people. You don't have to take them to bed, but you never know what someone can say or do to make you appreciate home a little better."

"Well, I don't know," Curtis said. "I think that can open the door to all sorts of things, and I don't want to take that chance."

"So you're telling me that you haven't seen a little honey on that new job to strike your fancy?"

"No, not really," Curtis said. "There are a lot of little honeys on the job, but I haven't been talking to anyone in particular."

Curtis turned away. He knew he was lying because there was one female he had seen who was different from the others. He wasn't overly attracted to her, but something about her piqued his curiosity. The more he talked with Galen, the easier it would be for Galen to see that he was lying. That he also knew. They had been friends for so long, it was hard for either one to get away with lying.

"There's something you are not telling me," Galen said. "But you know the truth, and whatever you do, you know that I am here for you, man."

Curtis decided then that he should leave because the more he talked, the more he would confess, and he didn't want Galen to know everything. Not yet. "I'm leaving man. I have had enough of your shit for one night."

"No problem, Curtis, but you're a little drunk so please take your ass straight home."

"Okay, I will," Curtis answered as he opened the door to go.

"Curtis, have you kissed her yet?" Galen said slyly.

Curtis smiled and walked to his car. Instead of going home, he decided to stop by the beach to clear his head a little more. He realized that he was tipsier than he thought. He took his shoes off and walked down the beach. There were no lights on, but the brightness of the moon caused the ocean and sand to light up. There could be no better night for lovemaking. A slight breeze blew, and the the ocean gave the air a salty aroma. Curtis was walking in the water and could feel the sand between his toes. He had thought about all the nights Grace and he had walked this beach. The nights they would lie there in the sand in each other's arms. Curtis thought no woman was more beautiful than Grace. He recalled a simpler time, before the kids. He and Grace were inseparable. People in their circle thought they made the perfect couple, and so did Curtis. Grace was everything he ever wanted. As he walked down the beach, he would pick up seashell after seashell and throw them across the water, breaking up the perfect reflection of the moon.

Suddenly it was his own mind that he no longer understood. He started thinking about the girl at work. He had seen her on several occasions now, but they had never talked. She was always alone. She wasn't caught up in the workplace drama. He had caught her looking his way once or twice, but he had not yet approached her. Just as Curtis tried to clear her from his mind, he looked up to see her coming his direction. What are the chances, he thought. Really, what are the chances? And he had to smile even as his hands erupted in a profuse and nervous sweat. As they approached each other, Curtis didn't know whether he would speak, but he decided to nod his head slightly at the last minute, and she returned the gesture. Once they passed each other, they both seemed to have turned around at the same time and just as quickly turn back, continuing the way they'd been going. Curtis was now sober and ready to go home.

When he got there Grace was asleep. He kissed her on the cheek, lay down, and fell into a deep sleep. When Curtis woke up the next morning, Grace was ready for work.

"Why didn't you wake me, Grace?" Curtis asked.

"I figured you needed the rest…after your extremely late night."

Curtis knew that was coming. Grace had always had a smart-ass mouth, and this comment was right up her alley. Normally Grace would wake Curtis up when she got up. She knew that he couldn't be late to work. Now Curtis had to rush to get ready, and this was her plan.

"So where did you go last night, Curtis?"

"I went over and sat at Galen's house and drank a few beers," Curtis said rushing into the shower. Curtis would never tell her he had drunk hard alcohol during the workweek; Grace would really get upset. She had always said that only alcoholics drank the day before they had to go to work.

"Since when did you and Galen become such good friends?"

You and Galen hadn't been that close since high school, and the only time you go over there is for your card games. Since when do you just go over and have drinks with him? She asked.

Still, Curtis felt he had to defend himself. "Grace, we have been good friends since grade school."

"I'm aware of that, Curtis. You just never go to his house just to chat."

"Well, I needed someone to talk to, and he was better company than you were last night," Curtis said as he jumped into the shower.

Grace didn't let it end though. She followed Curtis into the bathroom.

"So did he have any women there, Curtis?" she asked.

"No, Grace, he was home alone, and we just sat and talked. Is there something wrong with that?"

"It depends on what you guys talked about. If I know Galen, he was probably trying to get you to talk with one of his girlfriend's friends."

"Listen, Grace, it wasn't that kind of visit. I went there, and we talked about old times and how it used to be. After I got tired I came home, and that's it."

I just don't think he is the person that you should find solace in Grace added as she walked out of the door.

Curtis was surprised that she stopped so suddenly, but when he heard the front door close, he was relieved. He hated arguing with Grace. He never would win by arguing.

4

The Catalyst

🔲🔲🔲🔲🔲🔲🔲🔲🔲🔲🔲🔲🔲🔲🔲🔲🔲🔲🔲🔲🔲🔲🔲🔲🔲🔲🔲🔲🔲🔲🔲🔲🔲

Curtis was now on his job for quite some time, and he was actually spending a lot more time with his coworkers than his family. Grace never seemed to be happy anymore. This was evident in the way she talked to him. She commented on his activities at work as if she knew he was seeing someone there. Curtis had started going to the karaoke night at Beaches, a local bar across from the job. Many people from work always went there on Wednesday nights to embarrass themselves. He always made it home before too late, and Grace would argue with him every time he came home. He had always invited Grace to come out and hang with him, but she had never enjoyed being around a lot of people, so she would decline every time. One night, Curtis decided to stay a little later to sing in a contest that his office had set up with another office, against his better judgment. The girl from the office had come over with a few of her friends. Although he didn't talk to her, he made a point to let her know that he had noticed her. When the contest was over, Curtis walked to his car, realizing at last that the girl had parked near him and had been behind him the entire time.

"Have a good night," she said, as he opened the door to his car.

Startled, Curtis said, "Oh, thanks, you too."

Curtis thought, she must have followed him out on purpose, but he corralled his desire to start a conversation got in his car and drove home sobered. He knew that he would hear it from Grace. It was almost two in the morning. He had never come home that late without calling to let her know where he was. As he pulled into the drive, he could see that she had left on the light in the bedroom. She did this just in case she had fallen asleep, knowing that Curtis couldn't sleep with the lights on.

Grace was asleep when he came in. Quietly, he undressed, turned off the light, and slipped into the bathroom. The moment he finished, came back into the room, and quietly got into bed. Curtis knew there was no way Grace shouldn't have awakened by know, but he wasn't going to question it. After a few more minutes, Curtis thought that he would actually get to sleep without and argument.

"Why are you coming in here at two o'clock? Don't you have to go to work tomorrow?" Grace said quietly but sternly.

"Yes," Curtis said and then hurriedly before she could say anything more, "but we all went over to Beaches, and they had a big karaoke contest against another office and they needed me. I didn't think it was going to last this long, but we started having fun, so I just stayed there until it was over." He hated the sound of his own voice making excuses as if he were a boy instead of a man.

"You could at least have called to let me know you were going to be late," Grace said.

"Why should I do that?" Curtis asked. "Every time I do, you just start an argument on the phone. Don't you think I would rather hear it once instead of twice?"

"You always have a damned excuse when you sashay your ass in here late," she said. "I'm tired of this shit, Curtis. I come home and cook for your damn kids. I clean this damn house, make sure they get their homework done, who knows how many countless millions of other things. This isn't fair Curtis."

"Grace, you act like you are the only one who does something around here. Hell, if it wasn't for me, we would be living in a fucking jungle, and I never hear you volunteer to come out and help in the yard. And when things break around here, I fix them. We both have our roles. Don't complain about yours, and you will never hear me complain about mine. Just because I decide that I want to go out every now and again and you don't, it's not fair to always complain. Now if you want to change them, just let me know and we can reverse them," Curtis said. "I apologize for not calling, but you need to be a little more understanding.

Grace rolled over, saying nothing. She knew that he was right. She had chosen a bad example in her argument. She was just pissed off at him for staying out late, and she didn't care what he said, particularly if he had a point. That wasn't going to change.

But she would have the last word. Grace knew that Curtis would want sex this night. It had been a while and when he is drinking he always come home horny and smelling like a brewery. After Curtis hopped out of the shower, he had jumped in the bed without putting clothes on. Curtis decided that he would try touching her, but he could hear her soft snore.

"Grace, are you asleep already?" he asked.

"No but I'm trying to get there," she said in a flat voice. "I have to work in the morning.

"What in the hell do you mean?" Curtis fumed.

"You heard me. I am trying to sleep, so you need to roll your ass over and go to sleep too."

Curtis was horny as hell after all, and he felt that one of her roles was to satisfy her husband no matter what. "You mean I can't have any tonight?" Curtis asked. It occurred to him that he sounded like a depraved toddler at the candy store.

"Didn't I say I was trying to get some sleep?" Grace's voice was sluggish and dull. "I suggest you do the same," she added.

Now Curtis was tied up, and that alcohol he had drunk wasn't helping. Whether he decided to or not, he let the wrong words come out of his mouth. "Well, just remember I asked you first," he said. He knew she was doing this on purpose, and what he said was purely out of anger, but it was too late to take it back once it had been said.

"What in the hell did you just say, Curtis?" He knew he had made an awful mistake. He could feel the onrush of guilt and injury, but still rooted in his pride, Curtis continued to stand by his words. "You heard me. Just remember, I asked you first." He was caught in something he no longer controlled. It astounded him. He could not believe he had said it again.

"I can't believe you just said that shit," Grace said. "If you have another bitch you can ask, you need to get your ass up and go to her and take your shit with you because you won't be coming back."

"You know something, Grace, if I did have another bitch I was seeing, I know I would get treated better there. I'm tired of you always telling me no when I want to have sex with you just because you are angry with me." Curtis got up from the bed and put shorts on. "Hell, you are angry about something just about every other day. I might as well have someone else since I ain't getting no ass here."

There. Now didn't that prove he'd had the last word? Curtis got his pillow and lay down on the couch in the living room. He knew that the night would only get worse if he were to stay in bed. Grace would never follow him. Things had been worse before. As Curtis lay there trying to fall asleep, the last thing on his mind was not what had just exploded between him and his wife. It was the little good night he had received from the girl that worked at his office. He smiled remembering it right before falling to sleep.

5

Curtis Breaks

🔲🔲

Although Curtis and Grace had been together a long time, had loved each other a long time, things between them were changing. They had till now shared two lovely children and for all purposes had been happy. If the last few years had gotten shaky, Curtis could reasonably blame his new job. They did what was necessary to stay together, but had good times and bad times along the way. As it goes in the bad times, you are either stronger as a result or you are destroyed. You either have the chance to correct your mistakes, or you don't. Unfortunately for Curtis, his mistake was neither foreseeable nor repairable. Stepping outside the bounds of a marriage is detrimental enough, but if you decide to step out and experience something completely unknown, it becomes impossible—the point of no return. He had never crossed the line with anyone at work, but he finally decided to ask her name.

Curtis had seen her quite often by now, though he had never thought anything of it. She seemed distant from the people around her, almost unfriendly. What attracted him was not even her looks, but her unwillingness to get personal with anyone at work. She would actually walk right by Curtis and not even speak. He found out that her name was Janice, and while she expressed no interest outright, Curtis felt something that he believed in. There was something just in the way she would look at him, the way she avoided him because of the wedding band he wore.

Curtis and Galen happened to be hanging at the park checking out the scenes when Curtis saw Janice one day. Curtis had not realized Galen knew Janice, but it became clear when he called her over and started talking to her. When Janice approached, everyone spoke, and this was the first time Curtis and this woman ever had a real conversation. She and Galen talked for a while, and then she left.

Curious, Curtis asked, "What's up with that girl, man? She always seems to be in a bad mood at work."

Curtis told Galen how often he had seen her though he could never bring himself to speak. Galen said that he had known her for a while, that he had heard she was very high maintenance.

"She really doesn't mess around with guys who can't do anything for her," Galen said.

Curtis looked at Galen and said, "Yeah right," as though it mattered little to him whether or not he could do anything for her, but at the same time, it was undeniable that he was intrigued by the challenges Janice seemed to embody. He wanted to see just how high maintenance everyone claimed her to be, and if a man like him could bring her down a notch or two. "I tell you, Galen. She's lucky that I am a married man because I think anyone can be gotten."

The two friends laughed. Meanwhile, Curtis's mind boiled with the possibilities. Even if it did not go anywhere, it would definitely spice up his life. Maybe the advice he had gotten from Galen would prove right, Curtis thought. It was the kind of typical day that has lasting impact. Curtis would change his life forever. As Janice got in her car and drove off, Curtis watched her. He couldn't stop thinking of her. Long after her car had turned a corner and disappeared, he was still staring at the empty street. After the day at the park, Curtis and Janice were a little more familiar with each other and started speaking in the halls at work. One day Curtis took the fatal plunge. His curious nature finally got the best of him.

"Hey Janice, what are you doing for lunch today?" Curtis asked.

Janice turned around in astonishment that Curtis insinuated that they have lunch together. She looked Curtis up and down before settling on the ring he sported. "My usual," she responded, without further comment.

Curtis realized that she was playing cat and mouse and waiting on his next move. He also realized that she was going to address the ring on his finger, because she didn't hide the fact that she had been starring at it before she answered his question. Coyly Curtis responded, "Well, I had an invite for a free lunch for two from a salesmen from my meeting to Antonio's, and I thought you might want to join me."

Antonio's was a very expensive Italian restaurant with a romantic setting. He knew that would be right up Janice's alley.

Janice responded, "I don't know if it's a good idea for me to be seen with a man that is spoken for."

Curtis smiled. He was expecting that reply. "Well I understand your hesitation, and my first call was to my wife, but she couldn't join me. I figured an innocent lunch with a friend wouldn't hurt."

Janice looked at Curtis, saw that his request was sincere, and accepted. In the upcoming months, they actually became friends. Nevertheless, Curtis could not get around wanting to take it further, to see what she was really about. Curtis recalled one day while they were eating lunch saying to her, "I am going to make you love me." It was another one of those times his mouth overrode his brain. Once he said it, he had no clue what had possessed him. By the time he heard it coming out of his mouth, the damage was already done. The great male sacrilege of putting stupid shit out there. Janice had looked at him in a strange way and said nothing, but he felt her curiosity. A few weeks passed, and the conversations continued. The lunches now took place daily, and overall, their friendship seemed to be blossoming within the range of business hours. He still had not asked to see her outside of work though it seemed to him that since the day at the park he had wondered about putting her in his bed. Spurned by Galen's comment about her being hard to get, Curtis had inevitably foreseen the final act as a feat, a hell of an accomplishment, and ultimately something he would attain. On the night of the Tyson-Holyfield fight, they agreed to invite people over to her house, everyone chipping in ten bucks for the cost of viewing the big event. It would be the first night of many that Curtis would darken her doorstep. The fight went the distance, and about the time it was over, everyone had gotten tipsy, including Curtis. The alcohol gave him the nerve to see what would happen if finally he made his next move.

"Do you need help cleaning, Janice ?" Curtis asked.

"Of course, if you can stick around for a while. This was your idea anyway," Janice answered.

"Well, I guess it's the least I can do," Curtis joked. He knew if she accepted his offer to help, it would lead to other things later.

By the time all the cleaning was done, everyone else had gone, and they were left alone. "I should get going," Curtis said. "You want to walk me to the door?" He was thinking about trying to see if she would let him touch her, but he was too nervous to go through with it. He had never touched another woman the entire time he had been married, and he was having second thoughts about his intentions. The last time he cheated on Grace was before they had gotten married. He really had not thought beyond his own ideas of selfish conquest, of victory. Now that it came to it, the only thing he could think about was how he could get out of there. The door seemed miles away.

By the time he reached the door, he couldn't even turn around and look her in the eyes. He already was feeling guilty as hell just being there. As he opened the door, Janice thanked him for the help.

"No problem," Curtis said.

When he turned around to face her and their eyes met, he knew she wanted him. Rather than respond to their mutual desire, he inexplicably chose to put his foot in his mouth and said, "Can I get a hug for the road?"

Janice responded with a hug, and before he knew it, they were kissing each other. As Curtis felt her body come closer, he his natural instincts took over, and he started to grind her. Before long, they were both naked on the side of her couch fucking like two dogs in heat.

It had been a while since Janice was intimate with anyone. She had decided after the last guy she dated, who turned out to be an undercover brother, she would take a break. She couldn't believe that she chose someone else who wasn't good for her.

Needless to say, Curtis didn't leave her house for a couple more hours. When Curtis did finally leave, he recounted to himself what had occurred in disbelief. She had been truly amazing. She had done things that Grace had never attempted—things he had only seen on those tapes he kept hidden from Grace. Oh Grace! It was not long before his mind turned back to his Grace. How could he take back the night, to reverse this feeling of darkness that was overcoming him? He had started something that would soon end his marriage, and he knew it.

Curtis and Janice began sleeping together at least three days a week. She did things to him that he had never experienced. The girl was like crack to Curtis, and like crack getting the best of him. One night when they were together and she was riding him like nobody's business, at around three in the morning, her doorbell rang. A bad feeling already in his stomach, Curtis asked her if she was expecting anybody.

"No," Janice said.

Somehow then, he just knew. At that moment, Curtis knew Grace was at the door. Something inside of him had been bothering him all night. "Don't answer it," Curtis said.

"Okay, but I am going to see who it is." When Janice returned, she confirmed Curtis's hunch. Hide as they both tried, the knocks at the door only grew louder. Apparently, Grace wasn't leaving until someone came to that door. "Listen, Curtis. I have neighbors. I can't let that noise continue. Before long I will have everyone on this street in my business, and that's not going to happen."

"Well, if you do answer the door, don't tell her I'm here," Curtis moaned.

"So what am I supposed to tell her about your car being in the drive?" Janice asked.

"Tell her it broke down or something. Shit, I don't care. Just don't tell her I'm here."

Curtis's heart was racing so fast he thought that he was going to have a heart attack. Not in a hundred years did he ever think that he would be in this situation. He sat there and listened to the two women talk for some time. Janice was trying to convince Grace that Curtis was not there, but Grace kept yelling, "Tell that sorry motherfucker to come outside."

The night couldn't have ended any sooner for Curtis. Grace eventually left after an hour or two. He stayed huddled on Janice's bedroom floor, not knowing what to do.

He left Janice's house finally and drove around trying to gather his thoughts. He went to Ryan's house then. Ryan had been a longtime friend. They were talking for about five minutes when Grace came up. He had seen her pass by and then reverse. As she pulled into Ryan's drive, she plowed over the hedge. Before Grace could get out of the car, Curtis ran outside to meet her. He couldn't believe what they were going through. The world was spinning inside of his head rapidly, and he couldn't control it. The conversation that he was about to have with Grace was going to be difficult. How could you face someone you love after being caught screwing someone else? What do you say to this person? Everything in him wished he had never slept with that girl. It wasn't logical. As they sat there and talked and he had to look in her eyes and see the hurt that he had caused, he realized that it was the last thing that he'd ever wanted. They weren't as close as they should have been lately, but she didn't deserve this. She was the joy and would always be everything to Curtis.

Grace started asking him questions that he couldn't answer because he knew that it would hurt her even more. After about an hour, he saw the hurt turn into anger, and she went after him as if to kill him. She started swinging at him while all he could do was to grab and hold her. He held her and continuously told her that he was sorry and didn't mean for this to happen. She broke down then, and they both started crying.

"Why did you sleep with her, Curtis? Why did you sleep with her, Curtis?" She asked him the same question over and over. They both knew that things would never be the same. Try as they may, Curtis and Grace's life came to a scretching halt. Curtis' guilt continued to eat away at his very being. Every day was a struggle for Curtis. Everytime he looked into Grace's eyes, a part of him dissolved. It wasn't long before Curtis would pack a small bag and leave a fraction of the man he had been only a week earlier.

6

Guavaween Night

░░

t was a Saturday night like every other weekend. The weather was perfect for late October. It had just begun to cool down. Janice and Curtis were checking the *Weekender* for an evening outing. There wasn't much they hadn't already seen or done. Unlike Grace Janice was always up for a good time. Their neighborhood was quiet, and both wanted something neither of them had ever done. They ran into the article about Guavaween, a Halloween celebration that had turned into one of the biggest costume parties in the country. People would work on their outfits for months to try to shine the brightest. It was one night you could be whatever you imagined, one night you could see from the wildest stretch of your imagination. Curtis and Janice saw thousands of people roam the streets in outlandish outfits. There were costumes from vampires to almighty God himself.

Curtis and Janice walked the streets tripping on the costumes being paraded about. The streets were crowded enough to lose yourself. Curtis had not wanted to, but it was something to do, and he had always heard about it.

This party took place in one of the oldest retail districts in the Bay area. The buildings were all-historical—most made of Augusta bricks. Most of the buildings had been converted to clubs, stretched one after another down the main street. Some had been renovated, but they were all made up to look as if they were aged. Every type of club seemed to flourish whether gothic or reggae. No matter what your preference, you would be able to find it at Ybor City. Curtis and Janice went into several clubs, but were more interested in just walking around looking at all the strange costumes.

One costume really caught Curtis's attention because he couldn't tell whether or not it was a costume or real. A lady had on a hospital robe with the back of the robe opened to reveal a fake ass perched on top of her own ass. At first, Curtis thought, damn, she got back, but the ass stuck out so far from the robe and looked so real, he couldn't take his eyes off the spectacle. The closer he got, the more he could tell it wasn't real, but he still could not divert his attention. He had fallen a couple of steps behind Janice and didn't realize it until something else had caught his attention. As Curtis looked up, he came across one of the most beautiful women at Guavaween. Her face was at once familiar and unfamiliar. Their eyes met amidst the crowd of hundreds. For a moment the only person he saw was her. It was as if everyone had disappeared. For about five seconds, they were the only two. He managed to raise his hand as if to say hi. She smiled and returned the gesture, and Curtis smiled as if to say, "Damn, I'm glad we met," although they had exchanged no words. Curtis walked away knowing there was something about her, something that would reunite them.

Janice's voice rang in from the distance. "Who are you smiling at?" Janice said.

"Oh, no one. I had just seen this really crazy outfit."

She shot him a doubtful unit as if to say, "yeah right." As they started to walk, Curtis glanced back where he had seen his new enchantress, but the parted sea of people had closed as quickly as it had opened. She had disappeared just as she had appeared. The only thing he could see was that damned smile for the rest of the night. No matter what he did, he could not get that smile out of his mind. He understood then that he would have to talk to her, to know her. The weird outing had been defined for him. It was his destiny to see her that night. Even though they did not utter a word to each other, mentally he had made a connection. Curtis had never believed in love at first sight, but since the night of festival, he felt he had discovered a connection with someone that would have been incomprehensible had it not happened to him, taken hold of him, and shook him. How could he feel this way about someone he had never met?

Curtis later found out that she worked in the same office complex, and he had run across her a few times in the café. He knew that there was something familiar about her face. But he remembered that she wore a wedding band, and he never thought he would end up dating someone already married. The Monday following Guavaween, she made her way to Curtis's cubicle and asked him if he'd enjoyed himself. When she walked up to Curtis, he recognized her immediately.

"It's you I saw that night?" Curtis asked.

"Yeah, it was me. You didn't know who I was when you spoke?"

"No, I didn't. I knew you looked familiar, but I didn't put it together. You weren't dressed like you dress here at work."

"Well, my name is Anne, and you still never answered my question, Curtis." Anne wanted Curtis to know that she knew his name.

"Well I had a pretty good time, something different," Curtis explained.

"That was your first time there?" Anne asked.

"Yeah, there was nothing else going on that night, so I decided to check it out. It was worth the trip."

"So you really had no idea who you were speaking to, huh?"

"Honestly, I didn't. I know I looked up and seen this beautiful woman looking at me. I had no choice but to speak."

Anne blushed. "Well, I just wanted to come and see if you had a good time. I have to get back to my desk now."

Curtis didn't want her to leave just yet. "Who were you with?" he asked boldly.

"I was with a girlfriend of mine. I saw you had your girl with you," she said. "Doesn't she work here in the building?"

"Yeah, she's on the fourth floor."

"I thought I recognized her," Anne said. "Well, I think it's time for me to be getting along. I don't want your lady friend coming by here and getting the wrong idea."

As she walked away, Curtis couldn't help peeking around the corner to look at her ass. She had one of the sexiest walks he had ever seen, and just as he got fixated on her ass, she turned around, as if she had known what he would do. He quickly pulled back into his office, embarrassed that he had gotten caught. Anne just smiled. The horns, it seemed, were starting to make their appearance.

From that day on, Curtis went out of his way to say hi to Anne. From the pictures on her desk and the ring on her finger, she seemed to be happily married though she did nothing to resist his flirtations. She actually even encouraged him. He never asked her about her marriage. If she wanted to talk about it, she would bring it up, he thought. As months went by, Curtis and Anne became good friends. They never crossed the line although it was in the same spirit that they often grazed it. They actually thought that they were soul mates and that they had been together in a prior life. His mental connection with her was there long before their acquaintance. Fate had brought two people together, each one uncertain about what a chance meeting would conjure.

Curtis had thought she was out of reach, and Anne had never considered a relationship with a man of his character. Purely by chance he'd caught her eye; purely by chance in the midst of several thousand people, he'd managed to raise his hand to say hi. Unsure about her response after all, little did Curtis know that some things need not be explored. What was so familiar about each to the other uncontrollably drew them to each other. For the same reasons they were not to be together, they were not to be apart.

Janice realized that the relationship with Curtis was fading quick. He didn't love her, and that he was only staying with her for convenience. She, on the other hand, had fallen in love with him. He was a complete person and perfect in her eyes. Just as importantly, he got along with her kids. She rarely brought men home because she had two daughters and had always been careful of what she exposed them to. But they'd bonded quickly to Curtis, and he seemed to like them. Janice knew that their relationship revolved around sex and eventually he would look for something else. Janice appreciated that Curtis was good with his hands, that he could fix anything in the house. She had been more accustomed to handling everything herself, not having anyone around to rely on. She spent hundreds of dollars a year trying to keep her house together, and in the short time Curtis was there, he had taken up all types of projects. It was a few months before Janice noticed that Curtis had begun slowly removing certain essentials from the house.

"Curtis, is it my imagination, or have you taken your clothes somewhere else?"

"Janice, I've told you that I was looking for an apartment, that this was only a temporary arrangement." He waited for her to say something, but she didn't. "I found an apartment yesterday," Curtis continued.

"When were you going to tell me, Curtis?" Janice asked.

Curtis knew that the moment he told Janice he was moving, she would get upset, but he had to tell her now. He had to face it. "I was going to tell you tonight, when I got home. Hell, I really haven't seen you long enough to tell you until now."

An awkward silence reigned the air. Janice had gone out of town for the weekend with her sister to visit their mom. Curtis had planned this carefully. He had selected the apartment weeks ago but hadn't been able to tell her. He knew she would be out of town this weekend, so it would be easier to move some of his things without all the drama.

"The apartment became available last Friday, and if I hadn't committed to it, they would have leased it to someone else, so I took it," Curtis said.

"Well, I understand," Janice said, "but you still could have told me instead of letting me come home, seeing all your things gone."

"I apologize for that, Janice, but I had to act quickly. I guess I wasn't thinking." Curtis hated lying, but he couldn't go on living the charade with Janice. He needed his space, and she wouldn't do anything to stop him. She too understood how long he'd been married and that it would be hard for him to commit so soon after the seperation.

"At least let me help you decorate," Janice said cheerfully. They both knew Janice had a designer's eye.

"Sure," Curtis said. "We can do it next weekend."

7

The Children

After a few weeks in his apartment, Curtis decided to reach out to his kids. He hadn't talked to them in a while, and he knew it was time to tell them what was going on. Grace told Curtis that they would talk to both of the kids together, and she would give him the opportunity to tell them his side of the story. Despite all else, Grace knew that Curtis loved his kids more than anything, and she would never do or say anything to give Junior and Leigh a reason to dislike their father. The night Curtis decided to go over and talk to his children, he told Janice first. Janice said she didn't think it was a good idea. She told him she was afraid that it would tempt him to go back home. He reassured her otherwise, and they agreed that he would stop by after his visit with the kids.

When Curtis arrived at the house, he felt as though he didn't belong there. It had only been a couple of months, but he didn't feel as though he ever lived there. He was definitely an outsider, and these feelings were his own doing. He decided that he wouldn't pull into the driveway, but before he'd put his car into park, Junior and Leigh were running out to meet him. He thought they must have had some idea of what was going on and that they would be angry with him, but Grace hadn't told them. The kids were convinced there'd been an argument, that their father needed a little space.

"What's up, y'all?" Curtis said. "What's been going on?" Curtis could hardly get his words out before they both attacked him with affection. "Dang guys, y'all act like you haven't seen me in years."

"Well, excuse me," Leigh joked.

Curtis laughed and told them he missed them. Grace was now beside the car. "Hello, Grace, how have you been?"

"I'm okay, Curtis, and you?"

"I've been doing well. Just trying to get to the next day."

"Yeah, I guess I know what you mean. Your kids really miss you, huh?"

"Yeah, and I really miss them too." Silence followed their strained conversation. Curtis realized it was in his hands. "So kids," he started. "Guess your mom has told you that we were having some problems and I just needed some time away." Their smiles dropped. They heard a tone in his voice they had never heard before. "So we decided that we would talk to you together to give you an idea of what's going on."

As Curtis talked, he could tell the kids were trying to understand why their dad seemed strange and different to them. They seemed to sense that this was more serious than their mom had let on. Curtis went on to say that sometimes people make mistakes, and some mistakes are more serious than others. "Some mistakes can't be corrected, and it causes things to change," Curtis continued.

It was a struggle to speak to his children. He looked at Grace who lowered her eyes from him. It seemed that she was equally interested in what he had to say, how he would explain his mistakes. When she did finally return his stare, her eyes were cold and vengeful. She wasn't going to bail him out of the shit he had gotten his entire family involved in. "Look, kids, I made a terrible mistake, and I don't know what the outcome is going to be."

Curtis looked over at Leigh before continuing. Leigh was the crybaby of the family. She could cry a bucket of tears over losing a water drop, and he knew that what he was about to say would deeply affect her. Curtis was most afraid that if she started crying, he would be right behind her. He took a deep breath and continued. "Me and your mom are going to take some time away from each other and re-evaluate our relationship," he added. In trying not to go into detail about what really happened, Curtis knew he was talking in circles. Meanwhile, his phone was vibrating in his pocket the whole time. Janice, he thought and tried to ignore it. This was much too important.

After another pause, Curtis said, "I got an apartment on the other side of town, just in case you were wandering where I have been staying for the last couple of months, and I plan on keeping it until me and your mom resolve our issues. I just want you two to know that no matter what happens with me and your mom, I will love you just the same, and I will only be a phone call away."

Curtis held each of their chins in his hands and told them that he would do all he could to make things right again, but he couldn't promise that their parents would ever be back together. He could see Leigh's eyes were starting to well, and he worried that the moment her tears hit her jeans, he too would be crying. As he reached out to motion his kids in for a group hug, he saw above their shoulders Janice's car careening around the corner. Curtis literally blinked twice. He couldn't believe his eyes. He couldn't believe that she had the nerve to come to his house after all. He looked up at Grace just as Janice was pulling up. Grace had her mouth open and a look as if to say, "I know this bitch ain't coming to my house!" The only thing Curtis could think about was how he tried to keep the truth away from his children, and now this woman would make her presence known to all.

"What in the hell are you doing here, Janice?" Curtis asked.

"So why didn't you answer your damn phone, Curtis? You trying to move back here or what? I just want to know so you can come get the rest of your shit from my house."

Janice was simply being true to her emotions. Curtis realized that she had fallen in love with him, that she was afraid now of losing him, that she had not been able to and would never trust him. He couldn't hold any of it against her. As ashamed and embarrassed as he was, he had to understand.

He said in a calm voice, "You need to get in your car and take your ass home."

He could hear Grace telling Leigh to go get her tennis shoes and bring out the phone. Curtis's mind reeled in lap after lap of what had just occurred. Janice was still standing there. He had no idea what to do. Janice wanted an answer from Curtis, and he was not going to discuss this in front of his kids. Grace was getting ready for a fight with both kids huddled and shaking behind her. Curtis concluded the only way out was to leave. Let the rest take care of itself.

"I tell you what. I'm leaving," Curtis said.

As he started for his car, Grace ran over to him and made for his keys. "You are not going anywhere, and you need to answer her damned question," she said. "Hell, the secret's out of the bag now. I told you that I wasn't going to tell your kids, but it's funny how things work out."

Curtis freed himself from Grace and pushed her far enough away to squeeze into the seat of his car. Before she could regroup, Curtis had cranked the car and put it into reverse. He knew that if he left, the tension would be broken. They both were pissed at him, but they never would have gotten into a fistfight. Curtis knew them both too well. Despite the trash talk, they were both ladies. Backing up, he saw Janice doing the same. She had embarrassed herself enough for one night. She flew by him in the opposite direction without as much as a glance. Curtis left the house and couldn't believe what had just happened. In his wildest dreams, he would have never imagined his kids would witness such a display. He was always respectful of his children, and this night hurt him more than anything he had ever experienced. He made it back to his apartment, clutched his pillow, and wept as his phone began to ring. He didn't care who was calling; he didn't want to talk to anyone. Curtis decided to turn his phone off for the night. It was the only way to get any rest.

8
The Meat Market

🔲🔲🔲

Curtis was waiting patiently on the other end for Amp to pick up his ringing phone.

"Hello," Amp answered.

"What's up Amp? Are we getting out tonight?" Curtis asked.

Amp and Curtis had been to a wedding earlier that day, and Curtis wanted to see if he would hang out while still in town. Amp and Curtis became good friends when Amp moved to St. Pete three years ago. He dated one of Curtis's friends and ended up moving in with her. They lived together for a couple of years, had a kid, and then broke it off. Amp moved back to his hometown but would visit every couple of months. They would always get together somehow. Tonight of all nights, Curtis had to get out of the house. He was still recuperating, barely recovered from the last run-in with Janice.

"Hell yea, we can get out," Amp responded. "Are we going to the meat market?"

Nicknamed the Meat Market where desperate singles came to mingle, the club was reputed to bring luck to every poor slob who entered its doors looking for love. Every time Anthony and Curtis came, at least one of them if not both got lucky.

"Yeah, I guess we can go there. I have been on the outs with Janice lately, and I'm quite sure she isn't sitting home waiting on me to call," Curtis said.

They agreed to meet at ten. Curtis knew that going to this club would probably result in a rumble in the hay later on. He had at least two females there whom he fondly referred to as old faithfuls. After the last argument with Janice though, it would be refreshing. As much as he had been unwilling to admit it, it was time for him to let her go, and if so, Meat Market was the perfect way to do it.

The club was packed as ever that night. Because Curtis and Amp were not regulars, they cruised the floor with the idea that every woman there found them unusual and appealing. It wasn't long before two females latched on to them, and the night began to take its own course. The four of them spent the entire time dancing. The only time they left the dance floor was to get more drinks. As the closing lights blinked on, Curtis heard what seemed to be a universal moan amongst the revelers. It was not only he who did not wish for the night to end.

"How about breakfast?" one of the girls asked.

"Where would you like to go?" Curtis asked.

"I know a little restaurant around the corner from here, but they are always really crowded this time of night," said Andrea. By her tone of voice, the group caught on that what she meant was that they go somewhere a little more secluded.

"Well I have bacon and eggs at my house, and we are not that far away," Curtis offered. He had understood the suggestion for privacy perfectly.

"Should we just follow you guys?" Terri asked.

"I want Andrea to ride with me, and you and Anthony can ride together. Is that okay?" Curtis offered.

"Of course," said Terri. "We will be right behind you."

"Okay, cool. Let's go."

Curtis could feel his phone. His suspicions were correct. Janice, as if she knew he'd gone out. He started to have a bad feeling about this night. She had turned showing unannounced at his door into a regular habit. If it was her calling, then her visiting was not improbable, no matter the time. Looking over at this new girl, he really didn't care anymore. He figured he could cross that bridge when he got to it. When they finally arrived at Curtis's house and the party was on again, no one even thought about food. Anthony had found some of Curtis's old albums and put on some classic Teddy. Everyone started getting a little cozier, and it wasn't long before Curtis grabbed Andrea and led her to his room. He made sure to tell Amp that if Janice knocked on the door to tell her he wasn't there.

"You mean she might come here tonight, man?" Amp sighed.

"It's a possibility," Curtis said.

"Man, I do not want to be in the middle of you and that crazy ass girl. I'm going to ask Terri to take me to my room, so if I'm not here when you surface, I will just see you tomorrow," Amp said.

"Okay, that's cool. I will take Andrea home when she's ready." Curtis and Andrea dissappeared into his room, and he told Amp to lock the door when he left. Soon after Anthony and Terri left, Janice knocked on the door. Curtis ignored the knocking. She began to knock again, and Andrea started to get a little nervous.

"Who is that?" she asked Curtis.

"That's a friend of mine. We haven't talked in over a month," Curtis lied. "I have no idea why she is here. I just won't go to the door, and hopefully she will leave."

Janice's voice rang out then. "I know your ass is in there. You need to come open the damned door," Janice yelled through the window.

Curtis didn't move. He had decided to wait this out. After about an hour of her knocking on the door, he could hear her walking through the yard. She was trying to look into the windows of the bedroom, but they were too high.

"Is she right outside of the window?" asked Andrea.

"Yeah, she is, but she can't do anything except leave."

"I don't know. She seems very persistent."

"Well, that's her problem. I am trying to let her go anyway. She shouldn't have come here uninvited."

Curtis's venting gave way to a queasy silence. Relieved that Janice was gone, Curtis puts his arm around Andrea. "Told you she had no other choice but to leave," he said. "Now can we pick up where we left off?"

From the living room, a sudden noise made them both jump. Andrea pulled the sheet to her chest; a petrified look crossed her face. "Is she in your house? Hell, it sounds like she is in your house, Curtis." Andrea started dressing, muttering to herself that this was one fine mess she had gotten herself into.

"Hold on," Curtis said. "I will be right back."

Curtis went to the bedroom door and, without opening it, yelled, "What in the hell are you doing Janice? If I wanted to see you, I would have answered the door." Not hearing anything, he opened the door and saw Janice climbing through the window.

"Who do you have in there, Curtis?" Janice asked. She had gotten all the way through and was now standing on his window screen on the front porch, fixing and straightening her clothes.

"That's not the issue, Janice. Why are you breaking into my home? Putting your ass through my window?"

"You just better bring your ass out here or I'm going into the bedroom," Janice threatened.

Curtis certainly did not want Andrea to be involved. He scrambled to the door and stepped out onto the porch, zipping his pants.

"What have you been doing, Curtis? Who are you in there fucking? I can't believe this shit," said Janice. She was a disheveled mess. "You are actually in there fucking someone, aren't you?" Janice looked back into the house where Andrea's shoes sat against the wall. "And she's white, isn't she? I can just tell by them shoes. I can't believe you got a white bitch in there, Curtis. Why are you doing this shit?"

Janice looked like she was going to cry. Her eyes were caked with black mascara like she had already cried.

"Janice, we haven't talked in over two weeks. I haven't asked you what you have been doing. I haven't asked you out. Why are you fucking with me, pulling this through the window shit?" Curtis felt the damp of early morning creep inside his chest. "At least let me put a shirt on," he said, reentering the house and grabbing a blazer from the coat closet.

"We never said that this relationship was over, and you know I haven't been seeing anyone," Janice said. She shut and squeezed her eyes as if a terrible pain had hit her, but instead of crying, she lunged at Curtis with both fists clenched. He just caught her and held her.

"You need to stop this and go home. Coming here isn't going to make anything better," Curtis said.

"I want to see the bitch." It seemed that Janice would embark on the five stages of grief at an accelerated pace. Now, she'd hit anger. "Did he tell you he was fucking me last night?" she hollered.

Curtis pulled her toward his open chest to silence her. "You need to stop now and take your ass home," he said sternly.

"I can't believe you, Curtis," Janice wailed. She had not budged from his arms. "You knew I was coming by here tonight. Why would you have this bitch over here like this? Why are you trying to hurt me, Curtis?"

Her voice was so desperate and pleading, Curtis didn't know what to say. He did not want to hurt her. To hurt had not been the motivation for anything. Despite her tones, her agitation, there she was snuggling in closer to his chest again, and Curtis told himself, "one must rule with an iron fist."

"Listen Janice," he started. "I don't know what you have been doing for the last two weeks, and to be frank with you, I don't give a shit. Now you need to leave before I call the police."

Janice's body turned rigid. She went to scratch him, kick him, kill him, and then just as quickly caught herself. "You know something? You are not worth it," Janice said. She started to turn away and leave the porch. "And don't you call me. Ever! Don't come to my house. Ever! I'm through with your ass for good now."

He could still hear the tires dig into his gravel drive and peel off. Curtis sat down on the dewy porch steps overwhelmed and exhausted. Andrea appeared beside him wearing his striped pajama top.

"I'm sorry I caused you any problems," she said.

"Andrea, this isn't your fault. I should have never gotten you involved in my mess. I'm sorry." He had to admit, she looked great in his shirt. As he kissed Andrea, all memories of Janice began to dissolve. What a relief, he thought.

9

Damaged Goods

C urtis called Janice finally as the summer began when it occurred
to him that she had never wholly left him. He apologized for the
scene, the misgivings, and the white girl whose name he no longer
recalled. She told him she missed him, and because she missed him,
she had no choice but to forgive him. They made up in every physical
capacity, sometimes at her place, sometimes at his. What was shattered,
namely, trust, could not be as easily mended. Curtis showered her with
gifts, left packages in ribbons at her desk, and though she always swore
and jumped with happiness, she never let down her guard. Hell, who
could blame her?

Curtis did not understand the significance of her mistrust until one
hot night in July, while helping a friend with home repairs. Melissa
owned a house she was trying to rent out and needed someone to hang
the doors for her. He had already told her that he would help her whenever she was ready. He called Janice to let her know where he was
going and what he would be doing. Janice, appreciating the deference

Curtis was showing her, told him to take his time. But hours later and he was still not done, she began her incessant calling, her line of guilty as charged questioning.

"I told you these doors are taking longer than I'd anticipated," he said hotly. "Look, this is my first time doing this, and I need to take my time so I don't mess up this woman's house."

It got annoying dealing with her suspicions all the time. Theh air conditioning wasn't on and Curtis was sweating all over the phone and was really getting frustrated with Janice. He told her he'd have to go because his cell phone was starting to beep because of the battery dying. She mumbled something or other and hung up.

Curtis knew these doors needed to be done before tomorrow's baby shower. If it would take him all night, he'd stay and finish them, Curtis told himself. Melissa had already told him that he could sleep on the couch. He finished the doors as the clock was approaching 4:00 a.m. He decided that he would lie down and get a couple of hours before he had to go to work. As Curtis slept, Janice and her issues evaporated, and he forgot all about the conversation they'd never finished. He figured she knew his phone was dead, and he would just talk to her the next day.

Instead, she had taken it upon herself to wait for Curtis at his apartment. Sitting there an hour, she remembered at three in the morning what her mom had taught her about the only thing being open at that time of night being a pair of legs. Janice bounced around until she was convinced that she'd take out the bottom glass on the jealousy window, put her hand in, and opened the door. It was easy enough, so once she was in, she turned on the TV and the AC, plopped on the couch, and waited like any devoted woman would. She dozed off and woke up an hour later outrageously pissed. She could just envision Curtis out there somewhere giving her stuff away. The pit of her stomach wrenched up, and she started to hyperventilate over the possibility of Curtis screwing someone. She ran to the bathroom and came back out mad as hell. She wanted to do something to his ass, hurt him the way she was being hurt. As rage took over, she began tearing the clothes off his hangers and littering them all over the floor. She wanted do what Angela Basset did and burn all his stuff, but this wasn't her home, and fire seemed not only inconvenient but overtly conspicuous. Medea, Medea, she thought.

Janice found scissors and cut up every piece of clothing in the house. She didn't leave one piece unscathed; she even slashed through his brand new Tommy loafers.

On the other side of town, Curtis raised himself, cramped and a little weary just as the sun rose above the trees. He still had time to go home and change before work. He instinctively felt for his phone. There'd still be a couple of minutes to check the missed calls. When he turned the phone on, it was ringing. Janice was on the other line, and she sounded haggard.

She kept saying, "Please don't call the police. Please don't call the police." Then the phone went dead.

Curtis had no idea what she could be talking about, and he dismissed it, rushing around the house to pick up spare nails, gather up his things, and leave. When Curtis got home, he saw nothing out of the ordinary. He could have conceived Janice busting car windows, but there, the car sat intact, if only he hadn't opened the door! All over his white furniture with gold spray paint, Janice had written CHEATER and LIAR. The place was upside down with feathers and slashed pillows, remnants of this and that, tattered scarves out of his former clothing. Curtis just sat there on the bed not believing his eyes. He couldn't fathom how this woman could do something so devastating. He plugged his phone in so that he could call his job to inform them that he would be late. As he plugged in the phone, he saw Janice's note. Crazy bitch, he thought.

Curtis,

This letter is to let you know I will never bother you, call you, or pressure you about anything again. You have hurt me ultimately and you know it. I asked you were you seeing anyone, and you told me no. Curtis, you could have and should have been honest with me. The truth hurts, but lies hurt even worse...

After reading this Curtis tried to understand what she must have been going through. Although upset about his furniture being destroyed, he understood that she was hurting, and people do stupid shit when they are hurting. Why didn't he just call the police, dump her, let them pick her up? Hell, she had left a note. He did care about this girl. How or why, he had no way of knowing. Curtis discovered the threshing she had given his wardrobe. He picked up and laughed at his cut up shoes. The only thing she missed was a shirt hanging on the back of a chair in the dining room. He decided that he would call the police after all. He would put on this one good shirt still left, go into work, and explain to his supervisor.

Curtis didn't speak to anyone once at the office. He dashed straight to his computer, logged in, hoping for some news that might counter what he had seen at home. He didn't expect anything really. Not after this. The girl in the next door cubicle rolled over with a smirk on her face and asked what was wrong with his shirt. He looked over his shoulder and saw the slashes. Janice had gotten to everything. Without answering, he got up and stormed around until he was calm enough to enter his boss's office.

Delores had just walked in. Curtis managed to explain in one breath what had happened to him. He told her he thought he had no choice but to call the police. She understood, encouraging, telling him to call if he needed anything. Curtis was relieved. He would take the rest of the day off to settle things. On the way to his car, Curtis got a call from Janice's mother begging him not to press charges. He dismissed her as politely as he could given his mood and hung up.

Curtis called and had been connected to the local precinct. They told him that they would send an officer out as soon as they could. He went home, hunkered down in the sea of disaster, and waited for them to come. He thought about all that had happened. He went over it repeatedly in his head. He determined finally that he deserved the chaos after the bullshit he'd put his wife through. By the time the police arrived, he'd decided that he would just report a break in, not give them any names. He would warn Janice about the next time. For the next hour, they dusted for fingerprints, took pictures, and asked Curtis question after question, but he didn't give her up. Before the officer left, he told Curtis that it was obvious that he knew who had done this, that if he wanted to turn her in, just give them a call, and they would have her picked up.

As long as she didn't do anything to cause more trouble, Curtis thought, an arrest seemed unusually cruel. He knew that she had kids. She did not need a police record, and he did not want to give her one.

Curtis received a call from Toni, Janice's friend, to discuss damages. The police had already told Curtis that if he took payment from the person who had committed the break in, the case would have to be considered civil in which case, he could never have her arrested. He told Toni that he insisted on her paying for what she had damaged. Curtis put together a list, applying garage sale prices to try to recoup some of his losses. He was aware that after he took that first payment, he would be shit out of luck if she decided not to pay him the rest, and he knew that the bitch was smart enough to have already considered this as well. After the first payment, Janice never gave him another dime. What she didn't realize was that Curtis had never cashed the money order, so in actuality, he had never accepted payment. All academic and irrelevant when he had already decided to take the loss and pray that she didn't repeat her actions with someone who didn't care about her ass.

10

She's Married

Janice decided that she needed to break off all communication with Curtis. She didn't realize that she had fallen so much in love with him that it had turned into an unhealthy situation for her. On the night she had gone to his house, she had left her two kids home asleep in bed. After calling him several times and not getting an answer, she hadn't been able to restrain the impulse to take a quick ride to his house. Perhaps she was jealous, but the actuality of his having another female with him had not truly been evident to her. She had just been so desperate to know where he was and what he was doing. She didn't realize what she had done until she arrived back at home.

"What in the hell was I thinking?" Janice said to herself as she looked in on her girls. "How could I leave my babies here alone to go out chasing some asshole that cares less than a damn about me?" Janice just shook her head and kissed each of her daughters on the cheek and whispered, "I'm sorry, I'm so sorry," as they dreamed undisturbed. If he cheated on his wife, what made her think that he would respect their relationship? As she lay there in the bed, she couldn't help but laugh to herself. How stupid it all seemed now to let her emotions get to that point. Janice arrived at work on Monday, determined to change her schedule. She did not want to run into Curtis in the halls.

Chris, her coworker, teased. "Not going to meet with your break room buddy?" Chris knew that they had been seeing each other but wasn't aware of the extent that the affair had taken over Janice's life.

Janice looked away from him. "No, I will be taking my breaks without him from now on."

Chris heard the hurt in her voice, and as she walked off, he said, "If you ever need someone to talk to, I have very large ears." He knew that this would get somewhat of a laugh out of her because he really did have a large pair of ears.

She turned back with a small smile and waved. As she started down the staircase, she could smell the cologne that Curtis always wore. So she had timed it perfectly, she thought. He must have just gone back to work. When she entered the break room, Curtis was getting in line. He had also tried to change his break schedule so that he wouldn't bump into her. Anyway, she couldn't let this guy keep her from eating. She passed Curtis without saying anything. Everyone in the café seemed to be staring as if they could feel the thick tension. One thing about an office or a small town, it doesn't matter how much you try to keep a relationship secret, someone always knows until everyone knows. There was already talk about Curtis's separation from his wife, and people correctly assumed it was because of his affair with Janice.

Curtis got his breakfast and sat down to eat, and before he could finish saying grace, he heard. "Is somebody sitting here?" It was Anne with the prettiest smile ever.

"No," he said. "Have a seat."

"Thanks," she said. Curtis hadn't seen her since the time she had come by his desk. "You know you are sitting in the seat I normally sit in," she said.

"Oh, I'm sorry. I didn't realize we had personalized seating arrangements in here," Curtis joked.

"Yeah," she said. "You didn't get the memo?"

They both laughed.

"I changed my break schedule today. I'm usually sitting here thirty minutes earlier than this, so I guess I am occupying your time slot."

"Well, I guess I can get used to sitting over here," she said. "The view is better anyway." After a few minutes of silence, Anne said, "So what happened to taking lunch with your girl?"

Curtis just looked at Anne and said, "We decided to cool it for a while. This will be my break time from here on out."

"Oh good," Anne said.

They'd start taking breaks the same time everyday, fast becoming confidants. Although Curtis knew she was married, they had never talked about her husband; it just never came up. Anne enjoyed their time together and told him the conversation was the best she had had in years. Curtis found her very interesting and very attractive, but he never wanted to cross the line with her. What inevitably occurred to him when he looked at Anne were all the pictures of her husband upon her desk. Anne began talking about how she wanted to start going to the gym because her mother was coming down from New York to see her on Mother's Day. She knew that Curtis went to the gym at least four times a week. She explained to him about wanting to look her best. Curtis knew she was hinting around. She could easily go herself.

"You are more than welcome to come join me in the mornings if you'd like," he offered. "I can lay out a pretty nice routine for you, and by the time your mom gets here, she won't know who you are," Curtis said. "But if you accept you have to commit to at least three times a week, or I'm not going to help you." Curtis took his workouts seriously and didn't want anyone disrupting his groove.

Anne knew that Curtis would be the perfect trainer for her. She reconfigured her children's schedules, and they started going every other day. Anne had never seen Curtis outside of his button down shirt and pants. She hadn't realized how toned and muscular he was. Anne liked her men tall and bright skinned, and although she would have never been physically attracted to Curtis, there was a certain confidence he had about himself that was beginning to appeal to her. His perfect set of arms, his chest, thinking about it was enough to send chills through her body.

Anne and Curtis worked out for months, and their friendship continued to blossom. She had noticed a difference in her appearance and was pleased that he had helped her fine-tune her body. After three months side by side at the gym, Curtis felt relaxed and comfortable around Anne. He would grab her by her waist to help her with certain exercises. Finding themselves often in compromising positions, they managed to remain civilized even as the attraction each felt was inevitably intensifying.

11

The Party

C urtis and Anne were working out in the gym every day together, taking breaks together, and lunching together. It occurred to Curtis that this was no longer a healthy or innocent relationship. He knew that he was attracted to her sensed that she felt the same. They talked about everything and truly were friends. When Anne asked Curtis to come to her birthday party, he wasn't surprised. But why she would purposely put him in the presence of her spouse, he didn't understand. The most logical thing to do was keep him as far from her husband as possible, right?

But Anne liked living on the edge, and Curtis did not know yet. Ultimately, they would have this very much in common. They were being drawn closer and closer into a web of deception, spurned by their similarities. Why would Curtis even accept the invitation? Maybe he was curious. Curious about whom she went home to every night, curious about why she would invite him to a function where he'd be obligated to meet her husband, mom, and friends. People say that curiosity killed the cat, but that same cat has nine lives, and he could afford to be a little inquisitive at times.

Curtis called Jerome and asked him to accompany him. Jerome was married, went out once a week, and loved to flirt with women. When Curtis told him about the women who'd be there, he was all for it. In the car on the way, Curtis briefed Jerome as to the specifics. He told him how he'd been feeling about Anne, how she was married, how they were going to meet her husband tonight. He thought Curtis was crazy for going, but since there'd be food and fine ladies, he was down with it. Her directions were clear, and although Curtis had never been in this area before, he drove straight to the house.

As Curtis and Jerome walked to the door, Curtis still could not believe he was going to go through with it. They found the front door open and made their way to the room where the party was. Anne noticed them immediately, and as she approached them, Jerome said, "Damn, that's her?"

"Yeah, dog, that's my Anne."

"Hi, Curtis, how are you?"

"I'm fine. How you are?" Curtis answered nonchalantly, suppressing the thumping heart beneath his jacket.

"Good," she said.

"This is my friend Jerome. He's my bodyguard for tonight," Curtis said.

"Hi, Jerome, nice to meet you." Anne turned to Curtis. "Now what makes you think you need protection?"

Curtis smiled. Anne motioned him to come with her. She walked him over to where her husband was talking with his friends, introduced him as her coworker and the person she worked out with in the morning. Curtis squirmed in discomfort. To him, gym time was quality time. That meant this guy's wife was spending quality time with him. Anne's husband shook his hand and seemed completely unalarmed.

Don't sweat it anymore, Curtis told himself. Next was Anne's mother. Curtis felt that she gave him a strange look with a glint in her eye, this old knowing woman. Did she know something? Curtis wondered. Maybe he was just feeling guilty. As the night went on, everybody began to drink, and the crowd loosened up. Curtis was trying to be tactful and not stare at Anne.

She was looking attractive tonight with her Baby Phat jeans hugging all her curves. Curtis had never really seen her away from work before, not to mention, drinking. Anne asked him to dance, but there was no way he could dance with her in the presence of her husband. Couldn't everyone see his magnetic pull to her? Couldn't they tell he heard every word she said? Didn't they see his eyes following her around the room? Stevie Wonder would have seen it if he were here, Curtis convinced himself. Anne got angry with him and didn't understand why he couldn't or wouldn't dance with her. He explained to Myrna, Anne's best friend who seemed to understand.

"It's all that vino," Myrna joked.

Anne and Jerome danced next. Try as he might, Curtis couldn't take his eyes off Anne's ass. He noticed her husband also staring, so this was an opportunity without incident. She was so sensual; the way she moved was driving Curtis crazy. He was filled with wishing that he was her husband tonight, that it was he taking her home. Curtis hadn't realized that this person with whom he spent the mornings sweating on a treadmill would entice him so. He wanted her more than ever. He knew that once together again, he would have to let her know. He convinced himself that she was dancing for him, dancing like that for him to notice, dancing like that out of her mutual desire. He had not dreamed it. He had not mistaken it. She danced for him alone.

When the song ended, Anne's husband made a beeline to her, ensuring the next dance belonged to him. He must have felt what Curtis felt. Curtis truly believed that every man in the room must have felt what he felt. Jerome came over to him at the table and said, "Boy, if you don't get with that girl, let me know because she's looking for something, and I'll give you one week to make your move."

What he didn't realize was that Curtis and Anne had already formed a bond. Curtis told Jerome that he would give him her e-mail address in a week if he didn't make his move, although he had no intentions on giving him shit. While she danced with her husband, Curtis still watched her, wishing he was the one holding her close. Curtis was so consumed with his fascination; he pulled out his cell phone and left her a message while she danced there on the floor.

"Hi Anne, I'm sitting here about five paces away from you, watching you dance with your husband. You are so sexy I can barely stand it.

You are looking at me right now while you dance. You have no idea that the conversation that I'm having is with you. Why are you looking at me anyway? You should have all of your attention on your man. I am letting you know right now that I have a serious crush on you, and tonight has only capped it off. I hope that you will not pull away from me because of my confession. I will never make you feel uncomfortable when we are together, but I needed to get that off my chest. If you don't want to talk about this message, just erase it, and I will never bring it up again. Hopefully you feel the same way though, and we can talk about it on Monday. Good-bye."

When the song ended, Curtis walked up to her, said his good-byes, and got the hell out of there. Because she had thought enough of him to invite him, she had to care about him. In accepting her invitation, had he made it clear that he also cared, that they were on the same page that would be only a matter of time before they were in each other's arms.

12

Back to Work on Monday

onday couldn't come quickly enough for Curtis. He actually
went to bed at 9:00 p.m. on Sunday night to speed up the
process. Curtis arrived at the gym thirty minutes earlier to be
buffed by the time Anne arrived. She loved to touch his arms while
they worked out, he had noticed. He had always received compliments
about his arms, and he knew that Anne liked touching them, even if
she did so accidentally. Curtis hurried and went through his express
workout, hitting all the machines that would enhance his body. When
Anne walked in, he felt a little awkward for the first time in their
friendship. He didn't know how she would take the message he had
left on her phone, and standing there, watching her make her way to
him, he hoped that she wasn't angry about it. Her arriving on time and
flash of a smile as she slipped into the shower room to change was a
good sign. That eased his mind a little. By the time Anne reappeared,
Curtis had already started to sweat a little.

"So you came in early today, huh?" Anne asked.

Curtis didn't want to confess why he'd come. She had to know that he'd made a terrific effort to work up a good sweat for her.

"Yeah, I wanted to try a different workout today, and I didn't want it to interfere with our workout so I came in a little earlier," Curtis explained modestly.

Anne noticed that his arms were extremely swollen from the work-out and moistened with beads of sweat. His forehead was just starting to erupt in perspiration. He just seemed to glisten. Chills immediately ran up and down her body.

"It must have been all focused on your arms. I don't ever recall see-ing them that way before."

"Yeah," Curtis said. "It's my new arm routine."

"Well, it seems to work," Anne said as she reached over and took and handful of his arms in her hands. This was the first time Anne had ever made it obvious that she wanted to touch Curtis, and it didn't mat-ter where—she just wanted to put her hands on that sweaty body and not try to hide it.

Curtis realized that this touch was more seductive than ever before. She didn't just grab his arm, but held on to it for a couple of seconds, and on her release, she made sure her fingers ran across his biceps.

"So I guess you are not mad with me?" Curtis asked.

"No, I'm not, and actually, I'm glad you finally made the first move."

"I have been attracted to you for some time now, but didn't know if you would have reciprocated," Curtis said.

"When I listened to your message that night after I got home, I instantly started to get turned on. I don't know if it was the wine or just hearing your voice, but my panties were extremely wet when the mes-sage was over. By the time I left the bathroom and got into bed, Ty had already gone to sleep, so I just laid there and imagined that you were laying there in bed with me, and I started massaging myself and had one of my most satisfying orgasms of the year."

Curtis knew that they were friends, but he would have never imag-ined that she would share this much information with him. He just stood there with his mouth wide open in complete surprise.

"What's wrong with you?" Anne asked.

Curtis finally broke his silence and said, "Damn, is there anything you left out?"

"Oh, I'm sorry, Curtis, I didn't mean to embarrass you."

But before she could finish, Curtis interrupted, "Don't worry about it. I'm glad you told me. I will leave you a message every day if it's going to have that effect."

They both started to laugh. All the tension Curtis was feeling about seeing Anne just faded away. This day would forever change they way they interacted with each other. Although they continued to abide by business hours, never seeing each other outside of work, they both knew it would be a matter of time before something happened. The flirting at work was very exciting, and they both looked forward to it everyday.

13
The Cafeteria

A s they sat down to take their last break of the day, Curtis and Anne shared an ice cream cup and became engaged in a very deep conversation. Curtis started coming out of his shell more and more with Anne. He told her that he would like to taste her and how wonderful it would be to stick his tongue on her clit and massage it thoroughly. Anne couldn't do anything but blush. If she had been two shades lighter, her face would have appeared bright red. Curtis had a knack for saying the right things at the right time. Just the thought of him going down on her was so exciting and so breathtaking that she could literally imagine how it would feel, him caressing every part of her body with his succulent moist lips. By the time Curtis finished talking, her panties were nearly soaked.

Anne had gotten so intertwined in the conversation; she wasn't paying attention to her surroundings. Then all of a sudden a harsh dose of reality came crashing down on them both. They were rudely interrupted by Curtis's ex-girlfriend, Janice, the same girl Anne had seen him with on several occasions. She appeared out of nowhere. He already told Anne that Janice didn't want him to be seen with anyone at work out of respect for their past relationship, and up to this point, the relationship between Curtis and Anne had been relatively innocent. But now, Janice was there, at their table with her hands on her hips, rotating her neck in that motion that black women have perfected, telling Curtis she needed to talk to him.

He had already told Anne that they had broken up a few months ago. Janice, however, had never really accepted the fact that Curtis had moved on. She had never wanted to go away, and now, she wouldn't go away. Anne couldn't see what he had seen in her. Janice was thin, had short hair, and wore glasses. She was just not very attractive. Then again, Anne had never slept with her. The only compliment Anne had was that she wore nice clothing. She knew how to put an outfit together. Anne could recall admiring her attire before she even met Curtis. Anne had complimented Janice once on her shoes.

So as she stood there looking stupid, Curtis and Anne looked at each other and fell silent. She began to badger Curtis about paying her back the money he owed her. Curtis excused himself and pulled Janice to the side.

Anne was so fucking pissed off. She felt disrespected by her even approaching them with that bullshit while they were in deep conversation. As they began to talk, Anne could tell the conversation was getting really heated because Janice grabbed his shirt as he began to walk away.

Anne started yelling, "Let's just leave, Curtis. Let's just leave!"

Curtis kept trying to create paths to get away from Janice, but she continued to push him and shove him like she'd lost her mind. Now the way Janice was treating Curtis was starting to infuriate Anne. It was so high school. She was ready to go over there and kick her ass. Anne went over to some coworkers inside the cafeteria and asked them to call HR and tell them there was a fight going on. Nobody wanted to get involved though, so they told Anne there was nothing they could do. Anne looked over to Curtis to ask him if she should call, but he was still trying to break away from the witch. She had total control of him, and that really annoyed Anne. Finally, Anne stormed out of the cafeteria, went to Curtis's office, and began telling his coworkers what was going on. She also contacted HR. When Curtis finally got away from Janice, he found Anne and asked her if she'd contacted HR. When she said yes, Curtis blew up and asked her what she was thinking.

"That girl doesn't need any trouble in her life. She has kids. She's a supervisor, and she needs her job," Curtis said.

"Curtis, I can't believe you are defending that bitch. She knew she had kids before she grabbed your shirt." Anne thought that Janice paying the consequences for her irrational behavior was apt and just.

"Why didn't you at least defend yourself?" Anne kept asking.

Curtis could only say that it was because he didn't want to make a scene. The whole time they were talking, he kept looking at Anne with this strange look in his eyes. For some reason her heart really went out to him that day. She saw a weakness in him that she hadn't noticed before, and at the same time, he demonstrated character and strength, because the average guy would have knocked Janice down. Most women probably would have taken that as a weakness, but Anne interpreted it all as being very strong, wise, and sensitive to a woman's needs.

All of a sudden and out of nowhere, Curtis grabbed Anne and kissed the tears that had fallen from her eyes. They had never been this close before. Anne looked into his eyes and felt her heart skip a beat. She had never felt this way before from a simple kiss on the cheek. As she stared in his eyes, he lightly kissed her on the lips and told her that everything was okay. He asked Anne not to go to HR, but Anne insisted and told him he couldn't stop her. He realized that he could possibly control the outcome were he to go to HR with her. Curtis gave Anne excuse after excuse not to go through with it, but Anne didn't seem to hear a word he was saying.

When they got there the HR rep that would have handled this type of problem wasn't in, so Anne left her name and extension number with the secretary and went back to the main building. By now they had been away from their desk for quite some time, so they parted company and promised to talk about everything later.

Curtis called her about an hour later and asked how she was doing. Anne had calmed down, and once he realized this, he started pleading his case again. This time she really listened, and although she didn't agree with Curtis's reasoning, she decided that this bitch was his problem, and he would eventually have to do something to keep her in check. Anne said she'd have HR contact Janice and Curtis directly instead of telling them anything.

A rep from HR contacted Anne a couple of days later and asked her about the incident that took place in the cafeteria. Anne swore to Curtis that she wouldn't disclose any information, but when confronted by the rep, she said the hell with it and spilled the beans. Anne told the HR rep everything that happened from the beginning to the end. She gave her both Curtis's and Janice's names.

"Anne, you promised you wouldn't say anything when they called you," Curtis reproached her. Curtis told Anne that she should have stayed out of it.

"Curtis, she involved me when she interrupted our conversation," Anne said. "She not only disrespected you, but she also disrespected me. And the more I thought about it, the more I felt I had to say something."

Although Anne didn't say anything, she realized that Curtis still had feelings for Janice and he cared about what happened to her. At this point, Anne was so confused about the way he'd handled the situation; she didn't know anymore if she had done the right thing. It was unlike anything she had ever encountered from a black man. She knew black men to handle conflict by running away and not dealing with them at all or by physically trying to intimidate the women into submission.

14
On the Radio

urtis was sitting at his desk when he received an e-mail directing him to turn to a certain radio station. The e-mail was from Anne, and although Curtis always listened to a talk radio station every morning that would discuss national issues on the economy and politics, he decided to humor Anne by turning on her station.

The host of the show was giving advice regarding a letter that had been e-mailed to the station. She was saying that the person who had written the letter was asking for trouble and that she had to realize that the grass wasn't always greener on the other side. The host said that the woman needed to seek out a good friend, someone who would be honest with her and take her advice. Soon after the lady was done giving her advice, she then set the listening audience up for someone she called The Decipher.

At first Curtis didn't understand why Anne asked him to turn to this station, but he thought about it, there had to be a good reason, so he decided to continue listening to find out what this Decipher had to say.

The Decipher told the host that he had a different idea on what the letter was all about and that this heifer had written this letter into his show knowing good and damn well that he was going to expose her trifling behind. He started off by reading the letter on the air.

Dear Angel, Jerome, Marcina and, of course, you Dave:

I hope you can help me out. I have been married for over fifteen years now and have three kids from my husband. All my kids are now high school age and require less of my time since they are all involved in sports and other activities at school. I am so proud of them, Dave. But since they are now doing their own thing, this has caused me and my husband to spend more time together, and the only thing we do is argue. It seems that we can't agree on one thing. I tell you the truth when I say I hate to go home from work at night, so I stay overtime most nights out of the week. By the time I get home, he's already had a beer or two and is ready to start arguing. He is now accusing me of sleeping with someone on the job. I think he feels guilty because he cheated on me a few years ago with this girl on his job. To be honest with you, I have met this wonderful guy at work who seems to understand me more than my husband ever has. We talk at lunch, and since he sits really close to my desk, we are really talking to each other all day. He really seems as though he could be my soul mate. Because of all the tension I am going through at home, me and my husband rarely sleep together anymore. When we do, he still satisfies me, but then this is cancelled out by all the arguing. The guy at work has never been anything other than a gentleman though he has expressed that he would like to see me outside of work. I'm really considering taking him up on his offer. I'm just afraid that I might really fall in love with him. Dave, I don't want to leave my family, but I am in need of true affection, and my husband just isn't filling the bill right now. What do I do?

When Curtis finally heard the letter, he realized why Anne asked him to turn to that station. It was as if she had written the letter. This was almost the exact thing they were going through. Now Curtis was completely involved. He was curious about what The Decipher would say to this letter.

The first thing out of The Decipher's mouth was: "I can't believe this woman wants me to give her advice on something her trifling butt has already decided to do. Listen, lady, your horny butt done got tired of your husband because he done probably got a little out of shape lately, and may not be as horny as you. You say in the letter that he still satisfies you, so the problem isn't making love, it's the amount of time your horny behind wants to. And you want to try this new so-called prince you met at work, if you already haven't. See what the real truth is, you still haven't forgave your husband for cheating on you, and now you are trying to find an excuse to get your groove on. Hell, y'all probably have been arguing all throughout your marriage. You just are starting to notice because yo freaky butt want something different. Well, go ahead—go out with Prince Charming at work, your soul mate. Hell, your husband was your soul mate at one time. You must have forgot. Just keep in mind, this man at work has never had the cookie before, so he will be anybody you want him to be until you break him off. Then see how much you guys still have in common a few weeks after you break him off. Now if you just want to give him some because you find him attractive, then just say that, but don't send in this damn letter trying to put fault on your husband to justify what you want to do."

Curtis sat there at his desk and listened in rapt attention. He hadn't laughed so hard listening to a radio show ever. He called Anne and asked her why her trifling butt wrote the letter. They both got a good laugh from it, but Anne asked if it was true what they were saying about getting the cookie.

"Anne," Curtis responded, "everyone's situation is different. I'm quite sure that his comments were true in most cases, but the two people involved have to decide for themselves given their own circumstances. Are you considering doing what he said?" Curtis asked.

Anne was quiet. She really wanted to be with Curtis, but she knew it wouldn't be right. All she could think about was the kiss he had given her. Instead, she said, "That wouldn't be right, Curtis."

Curtis could tell that the guy on the radio had given her something to think about, and although they laughed about it, she really felt bad about what she was thinking. The show became Curtis's new favorite.

15

The Naked Room

One day Curtis invited Anne over for lunch. He made chicken breast on his George Foreman grill with a side of broccoli. It was so delicious, Anne thought. This was the type of person he was. He was always willing to please her no matter what. He was the kind of man who liked to wine and dine his woman. He was proud to show Anne how much he liked to cook. They were finishing up and talking as usual when it seemed that they were frozen, staring into each other's eyes and thinking on the same lines. Anne looked at his lips and licked hers, and before they knew it, they were kissing each other softly and tenderly. Anne's whole body caught on fire. They knew that this would be a deciding moment in their relationship. They either would go back to work and continue this relationship on a platonic level or let their emotions take over and go to a place they had never gone before together.

Knowing all of this in the back of her mind, Anne kept kissing him with more and more passion. Her feelings for Curtis were mental and physical. The heat was rising—the fire threatening to burn them both.

Anne knew they needed to put the fire out. Curtis was touching her body in all the right places, and as their bodies were pressed upon each other, she could feel his nature rise and press against her pelvic area. As they were standing there kissing, Anne couldn't remember exactly what happened, but she remembered moving backward, not sure if Curtis was pushing her or she was pulling him but that somehow, they were heading in the direction of the sofa. By the time they made it to the sofa, both of their shoes had been dislodged from their feet, and they fell onto the couch in slow motion, his body bent and excitable on top of hers. By this time, there was no turning back. Anne knew they were going to do the unthinkable, the unimaginable.

Then Curtis got up from the couch, took her hand, and motioned toward his bedroom. Anne followed him with great anticipation on what was about to happen. This wasn't the most attractive room in the apartment, but it would become the room in which emotional stability grew within Curtis and Anne. It was dark and gloomy with one small window, which was never opened. The other window had an air conditioner placed inside of it. There was a ceiling fan above that made a clicking sound like a clock ticking whenever it was on. Curtis never turned it off so the sound tuned itself out. There was green leather furniture from the 70s that did not blend in well with the rest of the room. A small ray of light would shimmy through the crack of the door that was to the rear of the room. The door didn't have any doorknobs or locks. It was bolted and Curtis never opened it, so it made Anne a little uneasy. She never asked any questions about it because she knew she was safe with Curtis. The room was always so cold, and Anne would shiver every time she entered though she quickly lost her shivers. There would always be little sounds outside of the room as if someone was standing right outside of the door talking, while smoking a cigarette. It must have been his neighbors because Curtis lived in a duplex apartment.

A lot was running through her head when she entered this room. Once they passed the threshold, their clothes just seemed to evaporate. All of a sudden, she realized that she was on lunch, naked, and in this man's room about to have sex. Anne's marriage seemed nonexistent. This was probably something she should have questioned, but the thought never crossed her mind. They were at a point of no return. Finally Anne found herself on top of a glass top dresser with her legs spread eagle and her nipples as hard as they could get. Curtis was sucking her breast and cuddling her body in a nurturing way. As Curtis sucked her breast, she began to moan, and she could feel her hands start to wrap around the back of his head.

The only thing going through Curtis's mind was complete disbelief. He couldn't believe that the married woman he had fantasized about for so long was actually in his room wearing nothing. He recalled a dream a few months ago in which he had kissed her. As he looked up into those beautiful eyes, he told her that he had kissed her before. She looked puzzled, and then he explained that he had kissed her in a dream a few months before. She looked at him and smiled. Curtis wasn't sure if she believed him or not, but this wasn't a line. He then turned her head slightly and started to kiss her ear softly, and this started a reaction that he wasn't prepared for. Her moans got a lot louder and she began to clinch him very tight as she started aggressively moving her hips. She reached down, grabbed Curtis's ass, and pulled it in her direction, and he could feel her moistness as she pressed up against his stomach. He then put his tongue in her mouth, and they had the most passionate kiss they both had in years. At this point Curtis was as hard as a jumbo jawbreaker. He could not wait any longer to be inside of her. He reached down and touched her in the spot that was almost dripping from excitement, and the only thing he could say was "shit." He could not believe how wet she was. He could hardly think. Curtis grabbed himself and slowly inserted half of his penis inside of her.

"Are you ready for this?" he asked.

Anne looked down at Curtis's penis and could not believe how large he was for someone of his stature. She whispered, "I have been ready for a long time."

She seemed to gasp for air as Curtis entered her. Curtis wanted to make this moment last; he kept teasing her by going in and out, but not coming all the way out and not completely giving her all of him. As he looked into her face, he could see those pearly whites through her slightly parted lips. She began to moan more and more. After a few minutes longer, he couldn't play anymore; he pressed hard on her pelvic area and went deeper and deeper into her body. Now her moan turned to *Oh yeses*, and *oh shits* as she dug her nails into Curtis's back, and this excited him even more. He started to move in and out at an accelerated pace, she laid back against his mirror, and the whole dresser started to gyrate. After a few minutes on the dresser, Curtis could tell Anne was about to reach her climax; she started saying, "Oh yeah, right there, right there." He knew that he had hit the right spot, but as long as he knew where it was, he could always come back to it.

"No, not yet," Curtis said, "not like this."

Curtis picked her up and took her to the bed, laid her down, and began to give her all he had in him. As he moved in and out of her, he could hear her start to reach her peak again. Then Anne made this sound Curtis had never heard before, and he knew she was on the verge of an orgasm. This turned Curtis on even more. He also reached that magic moment, and it was worth being late to work for the rest of the year. They both had cum at the same time, and as Curtis released his fluids, his toes curled up into little balls on the ends of his feet with the feeling that it would last forever.

Although she was happy that Curtis had this wonderful experience, she was even more pleased when she saw that he still had an erection. She then turned over, got on top of him, and started to screw his brains out. After a few minutes she became quiet, and all of a sudden she let out that unusual grunt again, and he knew she was exploding with sheer excitement. She began to shake, and then she was completely still. Curtis couldn't believe she had achieved two orgasms on their lunch break. He was also multiorgasmic, but not in such a brief time. They lay there a few moments more and looked at each other as if to say, "We did it." So the story goes that whenever they entered the naked room; their inhibitions went and then their clothes.

16

Hard to Leave

A nne knew in her heart she had fallen in love with Curtis, but the fact that she was married made her feel guilty every day she went home to Ty. She would spend eight hours a day with Curtis, and every time they were alone, they would steal a kiss or two. They even went as far as making love in the parking garage on several occasions. This was the most excitement in Anne's life in over fifteen years, and she was enjoying every minute if it. She wanted to be with Curtis and share every aspect of his life, but she couldn't do it. She considered leaving Ty, but they had been married for ten years. And she didn't know if the grass would be greener on the other side or if when she got there, it'd turn out to be just a pile of dirt.

She had always heard about women who cheated on their husbands, never thinking she would be one of them. She knew that she would never judge anyone ever again, even as they continued to judge her. She would get funny stares when walking by cubicles at work, and when she walked up on her friends at the lunch table, they would stop talking or try to change the conversation. It was obvious that they were talking about her. Eventually she started to distance herself from some of her coworkers and just hung out with one of her best friends. Myrna knew that Anne was seeing Curtis and would try to give Anne her advice. She had been in a work relationship, and it ended her marriage. She understood how this man could be so in tuned with Anne.

"Anne, you know I love you, and I would never do anything to mislead you, but just be careful. Curtis seems so right because you are not with him 24/7, so he can exhaust all of his emotions when he is with you," Myrna said. "But when you go home, he doesn't have to worry about the things on your plate, like getting the kids ready for school or cleaning the house or the credit card bills. These are the things that put marriages through the difficult times, and it makes it hard."

"But every time I have a problem, Curtis is always right there for me to solve it. I sometimes wonder if I'm a burden to him because I can hear myself complain and whine about things that are so minute, and he comes up with a clear-cut resolution. I often wonder what kind of future Curtis sees in us. Why he is even bothered with my preexisting relationship and me," Anne lamented.

"I'm telling you, girl, if you two did get together on a permanent basis, I guarantee you that you would see a different person."

Anne knew it was unfair for Curtis to be in such a situation, and even though he had decided six months ago that he was okay with it, she still believed that he deserved better. Despite her having this affair, Anne still had a conscience. She used to tell Curtis that if she got struck by lightning, it would be for good reason. She really hated the thought of sneaking around to see Curtis. Every chance she got, Anne would call him and speak freely whenever she was home alone and let him know that she missed him and couldn't stand another night away from him.

But she continually punished herself. "I am married and not the least bit single, and all I'm doing is pumping him up with empty thoughts," she'd say.

She would try to convince herself to end the affair. She would tell Curtis how bad it was at home, and that she was leaving her husband. Sometimes she just wanted Ty to hit her or call her a name that would penetrate deep into her soul so she could say, "That's it, dammit, I'm leaving". She spent every day looking for an excuse, a way out. Anne recalled a time when Ty did these things. If only he tried that shit now, she thought. If she had a Curtis in her life to stick by her once she made her decision to leave, she'd leave in a flash. Anne figured out Ty's code to his cell phone messages and checked it periodically for any signs of infidelity. The nerve of me, she thought. Every time she would check it, a queasy feeling came to her, just thinking of listening to another woman on the other end saying how good he was in bed last night and how she can't wait to see him again so that he could make her scream his name out loud over and over and over. Anne really didn't want to hear that kind of a message, or did she? But it would give her validity in her own secret relationship.

17

Motherly Advice

▌n Anne's house, the Saturday morning ritual was to clean the house. It had passed from generation to generation to scrub and wash every Saturday. Her mother had always had her and her brother clean the house from top to bottom. Anne's mom's house was nearly always spotless. Anne's mother had raised her and her brother to make good grades, keep a clean house, and respect their elders. It was embedded in them to treat people with respect and to have good morals and standards and apply them to every aspect of their lives. When they were little and she would take them to visit relatives or friends, they were constantly reminded of two things: do not put your hands on the walls and do not accept anything unless I allow it.

"If you wanted to see her turn ugly and embarrass you in front of anyone, then act like you were hungry and don't have manners. That's when you were humiliated right where you stood," Anne recalled fondly.

Anne could tell her mother about anything. Sometimes she held back on the negative issues between her and Ty so as not to worry her or vindicate her parents' first impression of Ty, which had been mostly negative. And these days, she mostly told her how well they were rather than the truth. Both Anne and her mother knew how much strength was required to stay true to their opinions as black women and how much must be done every-day to make a difference. As she loaded the white clothes in the washer, she suddenly felt the urge to tell her mother about what was going on in her life. Anne knew her mother wouldn't approve at all, but at least, she could give her some advice for dealing with the situation.

Anne picked up the phone and headed to another room where she could cry in peace and quiet. She knew the moment she started talking to her mom, the tears would flow. The phone rang and rang before her mother's serene voice answered, "Hello."

"Hi mom, how are you?"

"I'm fine, baby. How are you?"

"Mom, I have something to tell you, and it's been eating at me."

"What is it, baby?"

Anne took a deep breath and said cautiously but with undisguised relief, "I have been cheating on Ty with my new friend at work, and it's been going on for six months now. I don't know what I'm going to do because I feel like I can't stop seeing him. He's such a nice, caring, loving guy, and we seem to share the same dreams and goals."

"Anne, you know what I'm going to say though I'm glad you called me to confide in me."

Anne cut her off and rattled on about Ty's shortcomings and how boring he had become, how he had stopped listening to her, how he spent time with the kids while he barely seemed to notice her anymore. Anne was rationalizing, and they both knew it. Surprisingly Anne's mom took her side. She began saying how men don't know what they have until it's gone. Don't know a good woman who's trying to work hard and then cook and clean. How these young men ain't good for nothing today, they will leave first and think later. Anne shrank in the background not feeling any better, now wishing she had never called. She ended her mom's every line with "uh huh" as if her mom's ratio-nalizing of her selfish behavior showed her the true light of cheating. It was hard listening to her mother, but what she knew she needed to do had to be done on her own. Anne had to end her affair on her own and by herself.

She woke up Sunday morning and somehow had lost her resolve, deciding that she was not ready to end her love affair with her soul mate who could make her moan and cry all at the same time. Who could articulately give her a snapshot of the daily news and still know how to lean back to Fat Joe, listening to The Terra Squad. He was so attentive and willing to compromise, and right now she had him at his best. He knew what he was getting into and was still willing to go the extra mile. Anne convinced herself out of her lust to continue the deception.

While she doted on his strengths, she could admit that, like anyone else, he had his weaknesses. For example, it seem like she always had to initiate, what to do, when and how while he merely sat back and waited. She could picture the times she had intentionally not called him or made plans with him just to see if he would ever say how badly he wanted to see her. Finally after a few days, Curtis had brought it up, but this time she made him pick the time, day, and hour. She could understand Curtis not wanting to put added pressure on her relationship knowing her situation. He was right to a certain extent, but Anne felt that she could handle the relationship. She just wanted Curtis to show her that she was important to him. Sometimes she felt like a prostitute although she was not getting paid for the kind acts.

The fact that she was making love to two young men was pushing her mentally. When she and Curtis made love, it was hard going home to Ty and making love to him. She never had turned Ty down before because she felt a woman should please her man no matter what, but lately she was so tired, and Ty had been so horny he been wanting to go all night. Ty had been flattering her, telling her how good she looked and how he was so madly in love with her. He'd say he knew that every man wanted to be in his shoes. It was all fine and good early in the day, but after Curtis's roller-coaster ride in bed in the afternoon had maxed her out, she felt like she was only giving Ty leftovers. Still riding out like a cowgirl on one of those old black and white movies, she, however, had given Ty no room for suspicion. Anne would get energy out of nowhere, reach the point of no return, and then finally cum like nobody's business.

Anne could be said to be enjoying the best of both worlds, but at what price? She was so emotionally and physically drained that when Ty slept out in the living room three nights out of the week, she was happy to get some much-needed rest. Anne sometimes wondered when this would all end. When would Curtis come to her and tell her that he had found a girlfriend and no longer need her as a lover? Anne so often wanted to tell him that they couldn't do this anymore, but how do you tell the man you love that it's over and we will remain friends? It was so hard saying good-bye no matter how hard she tried.

18

Anne's Confession

When I first got married, I was truly in love without regrets. My life was absolutely complete. I had already had my first child and then, eleven months later, was having the second and fourteen months later, the third. Things were happening so fast for me that I didn't know if I was coming or going. My husband and I hadn't even begun to live our new lives together. I really didn't know much about him, the things he liked, or what he enjoyed doing. Our lives were consumed with the children.

The first year of our marriage was when the ugly creature's head popped up named infidelity. Yes, my knight in shining armor in whom I had put all my trust, faith, and loyalty cheated on me with another woman. The pain was extraordinary, and I couldn't think straight. Every part of my body was an emotional wreck. I asked, "Why me? I am so loving, caring, considerate, and beautiful. How could he do this to me?" Those questions ran across my mind everyday until I had to get his ass back. I cheated on him just to feel good about myself. Did I really feel good about cheating on the man I loved because he cheated on me? Not really, but my imaturity made sure that I got him back anyway.

I went out to a club and met my high school friend. We had been drinking, dancing all night, and enjoying each other's company. It was very refreshing seeing him again. He was looking so damn cute in his Lee jeans, long blue shirt with a baseball jersey over it, and NY Yankee baseball cap. He was as smooth as smooth could get. I remembered being so crazy about him in high school. I never wanted to be his girl-friend because he had had too many girls all over the place. By the time he reached twenty-five, he had at least eight illegitimate kids and eight different baby mamas. His personal life really didn't concern me much. There was something about him. Yes, He made me so crazy when I was around him. Floyd Fisher was his name, and he would be the man that I would cheat with. I made up my mind that he would be the one. That night there were so many people at the club and I knew almost 80 percent of them. I was looking rather hot and sexy and wanting the attention of every male in the place. I felt that all eyes were looking at me and my provocative way of dancing. I had the attention of every girl's boyfriend or husband in the place. I felt the vibes, and it felt pretty damned good. At this point in my life, I was looking for someone to fill the void. I had been cheated on and my self-esteem was shot. I had to pull it back up with every inch of my body's potential. That's what I used my body for. I used my body like it was a five-foot-five slinky, going back and fourth, in and out, round and round like a spinning top. My beauty enhanced my body and its curves and motions. Everything complimented itself in a way that was so instinctive and natural. I loved the way I was feeling that night.

"Baby, come back to my place." I knew that Floyd would ask me this. He had been giving me special attention all night, and I had all but told him I wanted to screw him. What about Tonya? I knew that he also lived with one of his baby's mamas.

"What about her?" he asked. "She's out of town anyway," he answered.

I couldn't believe that I was considering going to this guy's house where he lived with someone else. Although I had no feelings for this guy, going to his house just didn't sit well with me, and as far I knew it was probably her house anyway. There was no way he could have his own house with all those kids. But the bottom line was I just wanted to screw his brains out for one night, and I didn't give a damn where.

"Do you know when she'll be coming home?" I asked.

"Don't worry. I told you, you'll be fine, I promise."

Why did he have to say that, out of all things, why that? I should have known that he wasn't all he seemed to be. We headed to Floyd's house with only one thing on our minds, and that was to get laid. I was so scared. But every time fear invaded my mind, I dismissed it with, "Ty cheated on me first, and I'm just doing this to get back at him." That eased the pressure a lot. I was able to get in the mood a little more.

As soon as we got in the house, we jumped right into the passion of kissing, touching, hugging, and stripping off each other's clothes. I was so ready for his thick manhood to penetrate my walls of burning fire. The emotions took off racing in my soul that I could hear nothing but the panting of my heart. He tore open the packet of the condom and began putting it over his penis. By that time I was in heat. I could have burned that entire room up with my body heat. I kept telling him to hurry. He finally inserted the manhood into my vaginal walls, making me squirm with eagerness as I began to move my pelvis up and down. My legs felt numb, and my toes curled into a fetal position. He was going so damn fast I nearly fell out of the bed. All of a sudden, his body dropped on top of me, and he let out this long gasp of air with a whisper of a moan and pulled out of me. I looked at him like he had lost his damn mind.

I was thinking, "Is it over? Is this what I've been waiting for? I can't believe I cheated on my husband for this bullshit."

It wasn't even worth my time or efforts. I was so fucking pissed off. This was a travesty, and I couldn't believe that all of his baby mamas were pleased with this shit. Anyway, trying to save face, I was thanking him for a wonderful time. I didn't want to hurt his feelings by telling him that he was a big waste of time and a sorry excuse for a man with a big dick. I got up immediately and went into the bathroom to wash and get the hell out of there.

Even though I told Ty that I had forgiven him, I really never did. I was even more promiscuous than I had ever been. Although I didn't sleep with anyone else after that, I was flirtatious and seeking every man's attention. I believe that my husband made me into who I am today and the reason why I have an open affair with my companion—the one who truly makes me feel loved and makes me happy. A person who tells me how beautiful I am and shows me in the same breath. I never felt that I would be in the situation that I am in, loving and sleeping with two men. How the hell can I get out of this situation? It's mind boggling to even try to make sense out of the whole thing. All I know is that I can't leave Ty and that I love Curtis. Curtis told me that I needed excitement in my life at all times, and that's why I'm the way I am. He said that I like attention and I thrive on being the center attraction. I agree with that to a certain level. I must admit I do like the attention from the opposite sex, but I also believe that if I were satisfied, captivated, and fulfilled, I wouldn't have a problem with wanting so much attention.

I am a very spontaneous person with goals and dreams. I don't want to come home to a man who drinks every day, sits down, and watches TV. If he won't take me out, it gets boring and dull. Sitting at home is not me. I outgrew my husband. We were supposed to grow together, but he stopped growing and I took off. My suggestion for married couples is to listen to what your spouse has to say. Take him/her out to a movie or dinner at least twice a month. Do something that's really spontaneous and motivating. Surprise him/her with his/her favorite dish. Call him up and tell him to meet you at a restaurant and make sure you change your name. It will make the relationship more exciting and worth fighting for.

I am so scared that Ty and I will not make it. I love Ty so much, but it seems like he's giving up hope on life. He has no enthusiasm. He's stuck on the couch, and life is going right by him. I seem to bond so much with Curtis, but I am also afraid that he will find someone better than me who will give him everything I can't give him, and that's being his wife. I wouldn't blame him at all for finding someone to be totally his. Right now he's sharing another man's wife. That's not fair to him. I never wanted to hurt him at all because he means the world to me. He is a very giving and unselfish person. Maybe if Curtis does find someone, then maybe I could be devoted to Ty. All I keep thinking about is that things with Ty and me will someday get better.

19

Curtis's Confession

I t has been almost one year since I became involved with Anne. We have become very close, going through ups and downs like average couples although we are far from average. She is a married woman with a husband who really wants their marriage to work even if he is not willing to do the things that will keep them together. She tells me that all she wants is for him to take her out sometimes and spend quality time with her, not just go through the motions.

Sometimes I wish I could be a fly on the wall in their home to see what she is going through or what she is putting him through. He has spent over fifteen years with this woman and probably knows her better than anyone. In the short time I have spent with her, I know that she is very demanding, spoiled, outgoing, motivated, selfish, and willing to step out on a limb to make something happen. Is this the person that is driving her husband crazy? He would have to have at least three of these characteristics to be able to deal with her in a relationship. I wonder why, if she has been this way the entire time, this would hurt their relationship now.

Why is she talking about leaving her marriage now after fifteen years and three kids? I was faced with this same decision over two years ago, and I chose to leave. I left a marriage of nineteen years, two children, and a nice home. I have a lot of those same characteristics, some of which Anne has never seen before. She has only seen the person that I have to be, based on the nature of our relationship. I have my flaws that drove my wife crazy, but she would have done anything to keep our marriage together if I had given her the chance. I made a decision that affected far more people that I would ever imagine. I still wonder was it the right one. There has been no good to come from what I have done.

I have been involved with people with no intention of committing, which causes more problems for me. I have, in some way, alienated my two children. Although we talk and try to spend time together, when I look into their eyes, I see that they see me as an outsider, and that is the most agonizing thing I am going through now. I seem to have no real authority with them anymore. Even though we talk about a lot of issues, a certain amount of respect has been lost forever, and being a product of a broken marriage, I can understand it.

For years I hated my father for what he had done to my mother. As a kid, I just couldn't understand how my father couldn't love my mother enough not to hit her or not to leave. I was one of five kids who idolized her and thought she was the most giving mother in the world. There was nothing she wouldn't do for someone, and now that I know her as an adult, she is still the same mother I knew as a tot. I asked the question time and time again: what would make my father leave his young children, nice home, and this wonderful woman? My question would never be answered. Although I eventually had a relationship with my father before he passed, I never asked him these questions, when we used to talk, I know he saw the same look in my eyes that I now see in my kids' eyes. I now wonder will my kids ever ask me why, and if they do, what will I tell them?

Now comes Anne, who's asked me what my intentions are. I have grown to know and love her in so many ways. I understand what she is going through, and I know that she is having a difficult time. I really value the friendship we have formed and wouldn't want to see her hurt in any way. So how do I answer this question? I think the question is unfair to me. There is no way I can put myself in the position to be remotely the cause of any decision she makes; there is too much at stake. When

I made the decision to leave my home, it was not because I was in love with another person, and I made sure of this. I told myself, I need to leave for me, and no one had a bottomline effect on why I left my home. It would be wrong for me to say to Anne that we would be together forever because life is too uncertain. We could be happy for two years before things go wrong. This would cause more hatred than anything. I could be the cause of her losing everything. She would be a mother who's left two daughters and a son. I feel as though the decision my father made thirty years ago is still affecting his progeny. The decision I made two years ago will probably influence my offspring for years to come. Anne, on the other hand, is not the product of a broken home, and I don't think she understands the impact her actions may have.

I already feel a sense of responsibility because I am the person she is in love with. This is the selfish person in me who has reared his ugly head and made this woman fall in love. I could have handled this liaison differently. I could have not gotten close, knowing that she was married. I could have made better decisions. I let my emotions control my ability to think logically; hence we are in the predicament we're in today.

To be quite honest, given the opportunity to return to my home, I would take it. I have experienced quite a few things since my separation from Grace, but have yet to experience another like her. She had her weaknesses, but the good by far outweighed the bad. If only I had given us more time and not have moved on so soon. Maybe if I had been a little more open in communicating my desires. I recall the deciding moment in our marriage. We were called together because of an issue with our house. The kids were at a relative's house, and we were there alone. At the completion of the problem, we sat there and talked. The conversation was uncomfortable, and the tension was so great, it could have held up a car. I know deep in my heart that she wanted me to make a move and try to just hold and kiss her and tell her that everything was going to be all right. And I know she felt that this is what I wanted as well. However, whether it was pride or fear, I didn't make that move, and based on our past relationship, she didn't make it either. Grace was never the type of person that would initiate sex in our relationship, so I knew that she wouldn't have this time. Maybe had she reached out to me and made an exception to her rule, just this once, hell our marriage was on the line.

20

On the Town

🔲🔲

Curtis has had the week from hell. His co-workers were all fighting with each other, and he had been the referee. The bickering was unbearable, and he felt like telling everyone to take a recess and lie down for a nap. It was the end of the month, and everyone was on edge. One should expect chaos. He normally handled dilemmas a little better, but this week was overbearing. He needed a night out on the town and so did Anne.

"I don't have any plans," Curtis responded. Anne seemed to always be the one to initiate the first call.

"Well, I'm a little stressed and just need to get out of the house," she said.

Curtis knew that Anne needed to spend some quality time with him, if you know what I mean. Every time she called and said she was stressed, they would end up in some kind of funky position later on.

"We can go up to the Motorcycle Club if you want," Curtis said.

He knew that the drinks there were really stiff and you only needed a couple. Anne knew this too because the last time they were there, they never made it back into the house. They started kissing in the car and never made it out. They met at the Motorcycle Club at about the same time. Curtis knew that Anne had to travel for almost an hour, so he would wait for about fifty minutes before heading out, and they would meet there simultaneously. Thursday night was Ladies Night, and the crowd was always thick.

When Anne hung up with Curtis, she had been excited about tonight. She was sitting at her desk trying to visualize her closet to figure out what she was going to wear. She started putting pieces together in her head, but nothing really stuck out. The rest of the day she was in a good mood and made up her mind that nothing will go wrong for the rest of the day and into the night.

"This is going to be my time to relax, unwind, and enjoy," she thought. "Five o'clock already and I haven't called Ty, shit."

She was really dreading calling Ty. She knew that this was going to cause an argument. She picked up her cell to call Ty, and he answered on the first ring.

"Hello, what up Anne?"

He seemed to be a little irritated. This made it a little harder for Anne to tell him she was going out.

"What's wrong, baby?" Ann asked.

"Other than this sorry ass job I have, nothing," he answered.

"What happened today?" she said.

"They asked me to stay late tonight because Dave didn't get the reports done, and he couldn't stay. They are always pulling this shit, Anne."

"I know baby, but it will be okay. Hopefully you can get that other job you applied for."

"Yeah, whatever. Hey, you are going to have to go to the game without me."

Anne had just realized that her son was playing tonight, and she'd had to be there. Lucky she didn't plan on going out until late. That's when the party really jumped off anyway.

"That's okay, Ty. This isn't the first time and definitely won't be the last."

"Okay, well tell Jr. that I'm sorry I had to miss his game, and I will see him when I get home."

"Okay, bye," Anne said. "I will." Anne knew that she had to tell Ty that she was going out eventually. And just before Ty hung up, Anne said, "Ty," in a tone that told Ty she was going to say something that was going to piss him off.

"What, Anne?" he said.

The way he asked her that question, she decided not to tell Ty she wanted to go out. "Oh, that's okay. We'll just talk later," she said and hung up the phone.

Anne pulled up to Jr.'s football game and noticed Ty sitting in the bleachers cheering him on. She was surprised to see him there; disappointed that this might throw a wrench in her plans to get out. She was just going to go out and tell Ty that some of the mothers decided to hang out after the game. Now she had to come up with a different lie because she hadn't talked to the other mothers. Anne approached him with a sleek smile and a happy go lucky attitude.

"Hi Ty, how are you? Is the team winning?" she asked.

"I'm fine," he answered. "They just started, and from the look of things, I do believe they will beat the other team."

"So how did you manage to get out of working late?" Anne asked.

"The meeting for tomorrow got cancelled, so it wasn't as important to have them done tonight," Ty said. Ty seemed to be in a better mood since the last time she talked with him. Now would be the best time to tell him.

"Ty, a bunch of coworkers are getting together this evening at the Martini bar and having some drinks. We've had a long week, and it has been very strenuous for us."

"Why tonight?" Ty asked.

"Ty, I haven't been out in such a long time, and I need an outlet or I will have a nervous breakdown. You are more than welcome to come if you want." Anne knew that Ty would never go out with her and her co-workers. He wasn't the type to hang out and go to bars.

"All right, I don't see anything wrong with you hanging out for a few hours."

Anne was surprised. It went better than she'd thought it would.

Anne left a little early and met Curtis at his house about eleven o'clock, and to her surprise, he wasn't dressed. Instantly she got pissed, but she didn't let Curtis know how much. He knew that she was a bit irritated because of the look she gave him, but he hurried and put on his clothes and they were out the door. Anne's choice of clothing was a tight-fitted brown skirt that curved with every portion of her body, black leather boots, and a see-through black blouse. It was a last minute, but it was cute. They pulled up at the Motorcycle Club where there were hood rats on every corner searching for fresh meat. You had to pass them to get in the club. Curtis stood behind Anne and made sure that he had her back. Anne was comfortable knowing that he was there with her. Although she thought Curtis had her back, he missed the fact that her skirt had busted open exposing all her goodies. The bouncer at the door approached Anne and told her. If she were white, you would have seen the red on her face because she was so embarrassed. She couldn't believe that Curtis hadn't paid any attention to her ass at all as good as it looked in that skirt.

Curtis had already paid for them to get in the club, but after the news of her exposure they jetted back out the door, thanked the bouncer, and told him they'd be back. Anne could not believe this was happening to her out of all the days. She told herself that nothing would go wrong, but it had appeared that just like earlier in the day, it would end up just as bad. Curtis assured her that he would fix the zipper and not to worry. He also led her to believe that no one could really see anything back there.

"Yeah right, Curtis. I had the bouncer checking me out so hard that he noticed," Anne said. "That's a thought that will stick with me."

Curtis and Anne hid behind the parked cars trying to fix her zipper. Every time someone walked past, he or she would take a second look as if to say, "Damn, what are they doing? Is he giving her head or something?" Well, it wasn't working, what they were doing, because she was very nervous and Curtis couldn't get the zipper on the track. They finally went back to the car where there was light, and Curtis still working on that zipper, finally said, "I got it baby."

Anne was so happy Curtis fixed that zipper; she really wanted to go and have a good time. She thought though it would pop open again the moment she made the wrong move. She was so petrified about showing her face in that club again. She was imagining that the jealous girls were laughing and the men were gawking to see some more ass. Anyway, they headed back into the club and grabbed a table. Curtis got drinks, and they were strong as hell. Anne sipped on her drink slowly, but the more she sipped, the more anxious she became about her skirt popping open again. Hell, after a while she was feeling so good she didn't care if it did or didn't. Curtis and Anne started bonding as usual, and as she looked at him, he looked so damned sexy she could feel him all the way. He gazed into her eyes and seemed to pierce her heart. Anne's nipples were getting hard, and her panties were moist. He made her feel so good, and she loved the attention he was giving her. Anne thought she could get use to this.

Every time Anne and Curtis came to this club, he seemed to know someone, and tonight was no different. He ran into several familiar faces, one being his first girlfriend in grade school. She came up to their table abruptly and hugged Curtis. She kept fondling over him and touching him. You could tell that this young lady was on some type of drug. Her arms were dangling in the air, and she just couldn't keep still. Every few minutes she would drop it like it was hot, and she would get back up laughing. She whispered something in Curtis's ear, and he would look at her wishing she would leave.

After about fifteen minutes, Anne got annoyed with her because even though she seemed to have serious mental issues she knew she saw her sitting there. Curtis cut his eye at Anne and noticed that her demeanor had changed. Anne started fumbling with her glass, picking it up and putting it back down without taking a sip. Then she started moving it in a circle. Curtis told Jackie to go away finally. He had already made several attempts to get her to leave, but she wouldn't go anywhere. Jackie asked Curtis to buy her a drink and he said no. Anne finally had to take control and tell her to back off. She looked at Anne with the strangest look in her eyes as though to say, "Bitch, watch your back," before walking off.

After the incident with Jackie, the mood Curtis and Anne had been in disappeared. They hit the dance floor. They danced to three songs and then headed out the door. Although the interruption caused a damper on the moment, the evening got better as the night progressed.

It had gotten very late by the time they got back to Curtis's house, and Anne told him that it would be best if she went home. Anne really wanted Curtis to screw her so good that she would have an orgasm. When they got out of the car, Anne was adamant about not going into his house.

"So why are you leaving?" Curtis asked.

"It's already late, and I have to get home. I'm already late."

Curtis promised he'd make her cum within ten minutes, and then she could be on her way. When Curtis said that Anne's underwear immediately became wet; she wanted to feel him inside of her so bad, she almost lost her composure.

"No Curtis, I am not coming into your house. I really need to get home, and you know I have a long drive." Anne pushed Curtis back, looked into his eyes as if to say, "I mean it."

Curtis realized that Anne was serious so he conceded. "Okay, Anne, can I at least get a kiss before you leave?"

Anne pulled Curtis to her and started to kiss him passionately. Curtis slightly pulled away from her and looked into her eyes and said, "You don't have to go into my house."

He had gotten her close enough to seduce her, and he started kissing her on her neck, without saying a word lowering his head to her breasts as Anne warned him, "Do not get me worked up, Curtis, because I'm not doing anything."

Curtis knew that he had a trump card he had never played before, and tonight he was so horny that he played it. Curtis reassured Anne that he was all right as he reached around and reached under her skirt to realize she didn't have on any underwear. Curtis kept lowering his head until he had reached her naval and then suddenly dropped to his knees. Anne couldn't believe this gesture and wondered if he would go through with it. Curtis knew that she was daring enough to try him, but what she didn't realize was that Curtis had already made up his mind that he was going to go through with it. As Curtis pulled up her skirt, she was waiting for him to stop and say he was only kidding. But she knew that if he did, there was no way she was leaving. By the time Curtis reached the center of Anne's body, she had gotten extremely hot. He could visibly see her clitoris as it protruded from her body. Curtis had never realized how pretty it was.

Curtis showed no hesitation. He began to message her clitoris with his lips. Anne started to rub Curtis's head in a circular motion. She couldn't believe that Curtis was so good at oral sex. They had talked about it before, but he had never done it. Curtis took her clitoris and started playing with it with his tongue, and Anne started to moan even louder. Curtis then started to massage the inside of her vagina with his tongue but soon replaced it with his finger while he began to suck on her clitoris. Anne couldn't take it any longer, she exploded in sheer delight, and her legs grew so limp, she almost fell to the ground.

Curtis caught her and placed her on top of the car until her moans subsided. He knew that Anne would let him get off as well. He slipped his penis into her, and she was still throbbing from the intense orgasm she had just experienced. Curtis knew that she had to get home, so he made sure he did not spend more time in her than he had to. He pushed in and out for no more than two minutes, and just before he broke a sweat, he reached an orgasm and slowly removed himself from her. She wanted to go on for another round, but she knew she had to leave. Curtis told Anne that he was happy that she didn't go into the house. She smiled, got into the car, and sped off.

21

The Sleepover

🔲🔲

I t was a Sunday like every other Sunday. There was no reason to think that anything would be any different. Curtis woke up knowing that he was going to wash his car, clean the house, and watch his favorite team play some football. His friend from out of town was staying with him on her visit. She was fortunate enough to get tickets to the game. When he woke up that morning, the ticket to the game was sitting on the counter top. He wondered why his friend had left them there. First he thought maybe she had decided that she didn't want to go to the game after all; maybe she knew how badly he had wanted to go and left it for him. These were seats in the skybox where all the food and drinks were free. Curtis had never been to a game in the luxury seats before. Maybe she had changed her mind and was letting him go in her place, Curtis hoped.

As he cleaned the house, he couldn't help but think about the ticket that was left on the counter. It was now close to eleven, and the game would start at one. Just to get there on time, he would have to leave now and beat the traffic. "She still isn't here. What should I do? Should I take these tickets and go to the game, or should I just wait it out and see if my visitor makes it?" Curtis decided to call Anne. Anne could be trusted for her good advice, and Curtis needed a reason to call anyway. Anne answered, surprised to hear from him so early on Sunday morning. Curtis too was surprised that she'd answered the phone.

"Hi, young lady, how are you today?"

"I'm good," she replied. "How are you?"

"I'm okay, but I have a dilemma. My friend left these tickets on the counter, and she still hasn't come to pick them up. I'm thinking about getting dressed and taking that ticket and going to the game."

Curtis had told Anne that he was having a long time friend coming in town, and she would be staying there for the weekend.

"You can't do that," Anne said. "Did you even try and call her to see what's going on with her?"

"No, I have not. I really didn't want to know what was going on with her. I just want to go to that damn football game."

Curtis knew he needed to call the friend, but he didn't want to hear it from Anne. He walked outside for a clearer reception on the phone. The sun was high in the sky nearing noontime.

Anne said, "If you were going to the game, what time would you leave to make a one o'clock game?"

"I would have left a half hour ago, but you never know what she has planned."

"You need to hang up this phone up and call her right now then," Anne said.

While Curtis was outside, he had decided to start washing his car. It was a typical Florida day in mid-October, no clouds in the sky, warm but not hot. It was a perfect day for a football game.

"I know I need to call her. I just wanted to call you and hear your voice first today."

"I know, but you don't have to come up with a reason to call me," Anne said sweetly.

Meanwhile Curtis's friend came around the corner on two wheels, pulling up in the drive and hopping out of the car nearly before it had stopped.

"I guess we talked her up. She just came to get her ticket," Curtis said.

"Well, I have to go. My husband just came in the room. I will try and call you later," Anne promised.

Curtis had heard it before. He knew it was hard for her to call on Sundays, but, hell, it was hard for her to call on Saturday too. Curtis continued to wash his car as Jodi's friends piled on the driveway to meet her. They were all riding to the game together. Joking with his friend, Curtis told her this was her last chance to unload her tickets for free. They didn't go for it, laughing as they jumped into one car. Curtis was left in the drive looking like a sad puppy dog while they had on their football jerseys, hats, and flags.

"Damn I hate them," Curtis thought. He finished washing his car and went inside just in time for the kickoff. Curtis really hated watching the game alone, but he was growing accustomed to it. By the fourth quarter, he had drunk a few beers and felt pretty good. When his friend came home, she found Curtis asleep on the couch. She had invited a friend to watch the second game, and they quietly tapped him awake to share the couch. He was still drowsy when his phone rang.

"Hey, what are you doing?" It was Anne.

Surprised and still sleepy, Curtis said nothing.

"Oh, I'm in your neck of the woods," Anne added.

"What are you doing? Where are you going? Why are you in my area?" Curtis kept asking questions before she had a chance to answer them.

"Well, me and Ty were down at the pier."

"So how are you calling me?"

"Well, he just got out of the car and started walking, and I have no idea where he is."

"Oh, I'm quite sure he will be calling soon. Are you just sitting somewhere waiting on him?"

"No, actually I'm on my way to your house."

"Oh yeah? That's fine with me, but do you think that's a good idea?"

"Well, I don't know what else to do. I have been waiting on him for at least thirty minutes."

"You know you're more than welcomed to come here until he calls. I'm just sitting around with Jodi and her friend."

"Okay, I'll be over in about ten minutes."

"Okay, I'll be waiting," Curtis said.

By the time Anne got there, Curtis was feeling pretty good. He and Jodi's friend had opened the bottle of Jim Beam and were doing shots. When the doorbell rang, Curtis leaped to the door and let Anne in. She already knew everyone there because they'd all worked together before. Curtis was happy to see her, and so were the others. He was just a little concerned about what brought her to him on a Sunday afternoon. Everyone hugged Anne since they hadn't seen her in a while.

"So Anne, what you been up to?" asked Jodi.

"Nothing much. Same shit different day."

"Yeah, I know what you mean."

Curtis asked her if she wanted a drink, and she said that she had already had enough. He could tell by her demeanor that something just wasn't right, but he decided not to dwell on it. Jodi brought up the idea of karaoke, which is always a good idea when you have had a few drinks. Everyone took turns at singing the song of his or her choice. Jodi sang a song that she always sang, "Fever," and in her signature sexiness. It was a game they liked to play. Jodi would sing and strut, and Curtis would watch and fantasize about taking her by her long curly hair, sticking his tongue in her mouth and any other opening in her body to give her the most fantastic orgasm she'd ever known. He looked at her like he wanted her all night, could and would, though it was clear they both knew that it was only fantasy play. While she was singing this song, Curtis looked over at Anne who didn't seem to be feeling it, the song, or Jodi. Curtis thought she was a little upset seeing the connection he had with his old friend.

Once Jodi finished her song, Anne took the mic. It seemed she had been struggling to find the right song the whole time Jodi was singing. He recognized the song from being with her in the car. It was on one of his CDs. For someone to attempt to sing a Kelly Price, she had to be confident in her ability. The first words that came out of Anne's mouth were, "How did you get here" and what followed was so remarkable. She looked Curtis dead in the eyes and sang her ass off. Midway through the song, she got emotional and started to cry. Jodi and her friend just looked in astonishment. If they hadn't known that Anne and Curtis were seeing each other, they knew now.

When she finished the song, everyone's mouth hung open in the same manner. Only the ringing of Anne's phone broke the awed silence.

She answered her phone and headed toward the bedroom. Curtis knew that it was her husband. She stayed in the bedroom a few minutes arguing on the phone, and when she came out, she was clearly upset.

"Can we go outside and talk?" she asked Curtis.

"Sure," he said.

Once they got outside, she became extremely poignant. She started explaining that she and her husband had gone to this bar, had had a couple of drinks, and he had asked her to have a threesome with him. He had already picked out the woman, a close friend of theirs. She told Curtis how upset she was that he had asked for such a thing and that her being upset about it made Ty angry, which she could not understand. And that's when he asked her to drop him off. She had waited on him for at least twenty minutes in the car alone. Curtis was completely blown away. Jodi and her friend walked by to leave, whispering happy good-byes. Curtis told Anne that she should call her husband and go pick him up. She said she had tried several times, but he wouldn't tell her where he was. She was getting really annoyed with him and wanted to stop trying.

She then turned her phone off and gave Curtis the most sensual kiss ever. She immediately got a reaction from him. He wanted to take her right there on the back of the car. But it was still daylight and that would have been inappropriate since there were a lot of kids in the neighborhood. So he turned her around, grabbed her by her waist, and led her into the house. Before the door had closed, they were already taking off each other's clothes. By the time they reached the bedroom, a trail of clothes marked their path, and they were completely naked as they crossed the threshold of his room. The bed was close to the door, and before they knew it, they were lying on the bed, their naked bodies intertwined.

Although Curtis knew Anne's weakness was caressing her ear lobes with his tongue, there was no need for this today. She was so hot. He could feel the moisture of her as he ran his hand across her body. Just the feeling of this pool of her juices drove him insane. He knew she wanted him inside her right at that moment, but he wasn't going to let her off this easily though. As he kissed the nape of her neck, he ran his fingers across her nipples, massaging them ever so gently. He just had to have one of them in his mouth. He knew that this would take her to a soft moan. Curtis loved sucking on her nipples, and he knew the she loved it too. He felt her pelvic area start to stir. He knew now that she was full of love's juices, so he took his finger, ran it down her stomach, played with her navel for a short time, and then inserted his finger into her honey jar. Now her moan escalated a little as she clutched his shoulders and slightly dug her nails in.

Curtis wanted to drive her crazy; he wanted to make sure that she was completely overwhelmed with excitement. She was now so wet he almost couldn't contain himself. Her pelvis area started to gyrate even more, as Curtis's finger went in and out. She would take his hand and put it just where she wanted it. As he felt her clitoris, she let out a quick scream. It was so hard. As Curtis looked down at it, he could see that it was missing something. Curtis being the person that he was, he couldn't let it go without. He slowly released her nipple from the clutch of his lips and kissed the lower part of her breast. As he massaged her clitoris, he stuck his tongue in her navel, and he could feel her shiver with anticipation. Finally the time had come. As he took her clitoris between his lips, he sucked on it ever so lightly while massaging it with his tongue. The moment he started sucking on Anne's clit, her moans became screams of excitement. Her pelvis was now in full rotation. She was grinding on his face as if he was inside of her. In Curtis's mind he was smiling, knowing that he was driving her insane. He would look up from time to time and see that Anne was clutching his sheets as if she was trying to fend off an attacker. Her eyes were closed, and all he saw was her tongue rubbing across that pretty set of teeth. Curtis then inserted his finger into her again, and she started fucking it. Between Curtis's finger in Anne and his lips gripping her clit, she could barley control herself. All of a sudden she got really quiet, and her hips were starting to speed up. As Curtis felt her tempo change, he changed to equate her movements. Suddenly she let out a distinctive sound; he couldn't put his finger on it, but he knew she was imploding with excitement. She wrapped her thighs so tightly around his ears he couldn't hear anything. His eyes were still buried between her legs, and his mouth caught in an open position inside of her. Shit, at this moment he could neither see no evil, hear no evil, nor speak any.

Curtis inhaled all the juices she released, as she trembled uncontrollably. He had done his job. As Curtis rose to kiss her lips she whispered, "I love you," as he stuck his manhood deep into her. As she felt him enter into her darkness, she raised her legs high, as if to put out the welcome mat. Curtis went deep inside and felt the warmth on the volcano that had just erupted. As he went in and out, she began to yell out, "I love you," over and over again. This just made Curtis want to put every inch of his rod into her body. As he looked down at her, the expression on her face was that of complete fulfillment. She would grab his arms from time to time and dig her fingers deep into his skin. This felt so good. Curtis also let out moans that he had no power over. As his dick went up and down her shaft, he couldn't hold his love gun from shooting anymore.

As he released into Anne's hole, he seemed to have sunk deep into her soul. It seemed to last forever. Curtis's arms got so weak, he slowly let himself down to rest upon her breasts. He kissed the nape of her neck and said, "I love you too." She smiled, and they lay there and held each other.

The moment Anne turned on her phone, it rang. Her husband had started walking home, which was a pretty good hike. He left a message on her phone and said that he was going to beat her ass. Curtis said that whatever she did; don't let that man walk all the way home. He finally told her where he was, but she was afraid to go because he had threatened her. Curtis told her that she should go park the car somewhere and have him go pick it up, and she could spend the night with him. She agreed. On the way to drop off the car, Anne called Curtis and told him that she would be meeting Ty at a gas station to talk to him, to see if he was serious about his threats. When she arrived he took the keys and drove off, leaving her there. Curtis had followed Anne to the station and watched from a distance as Ty pulled into a curb, waiting to see who would pick Anne up. Curtis told her he would call her a cab and see if Ty would follow it. The cab finally took her to Walmart where Curtis picked her up and took her back to his house. They lay down, made love again, and fell asleep. Curtis and Anne both knew that tomorrow was going to be different. Everything was going to change. One thing was for sure. She knew she had to go home eventually.

22

What a scare

T he first time that Curtis and Anne slept together, they had used a condom. Every time after, they had not. It might have been a naïve thing to say on Anne's part, but as far as Anne knew, Curtis wasn't sleeping with anyone but her. At least, that's what he told her, and she believed him. Curtis promised Anne that if he slept with anyone he would let her know. He told her that he would give her the opportunity to decide to stay with him or not. Anne knew that that time was fast approaching, but she stayed focused on the present and on his loyalty. She knew and trusted that he would tell her if he was having sexual relationships with other women. He had never lied to her before, so she didn't have any reason not to believe him. The feeling of not having latex up inside of her was so great. And besides, his dick was so overwhelmingly large, she couldn't take a thick piece of rubber on top of it. It was not normal for a man to be that endowed, but it was so good, Anne felt only grateful and blessed. She hadn't used a rubber in all the many years that she was with Ty. She had forgotten how they felt until that day that Curtis wore one. After that day, it felt so real and natural for him to insert his penis in her raw as can be. There should be no condom for opened souls such as theirs were. The mutual bond that formulated between the two of them made every night together magical. The lovemaking was just a small piece of their bond. It was the whole connection of their hearts and minds in the end. The lovemaking was just the icing on the cake.

Lately though in the mornings, Anne had been experiencing pains in her abdomen and feeling sick. It was the scariest thing to experience, and she knew it wasn't time for her monthly to come on because it had already come on. She would slump over in agony, but as she would begin to really feel the pain, it went away. She browsed the web to see what was causing this strange ache in her stomach and what was caus- ing her to urinate every ten minutes. At work, she'd started keeping track of how many times she'd gone to the bathroom. Within an hour she had gone three times. It got so bad that the lower part of her stom- ach would incur this heavy pulsating pressure that was more annoying than painful. She found out that her symptoms sounded like those of a urinary tract infection. It was easy enough to remedy. She hadn't been to the OB-GYN since her last pap smear, and she thought that from what she'd read online, she'd cure it herself. Moreover, Anne was afraid of having something that she didn't want to face. She would have told Ty about it, but he didn't comment on anything that she would discuss with him, so she dismissed her physical aliment as well.

For whatever reason, she never mentioned the infection to Curtis. What Curtis and Anne did talk about was an issue that occurred after they made love and she had had an orgasm. Anne had started to bleed afterward. Curtis even looked it up on the Internet, and one site claimed that Anne could be having orgasms that were so intense that the blood vessels were popping causing her to bleed after sex. He could tell it made her nervous. The bleeding had never occurred with Ty.

To try to cure herself of the tract infection, Anne took advice from her girlfriend. Anne never figured she would take medical advice from a dental hygienist, but she did. Apparently, Anne's girlfriend was more familiar with the infection than she would have liked. Anne went and got an Uri stat from Walgreens. She took the antibiotics her girlfriend gave her to internally clear the infection and took the prescription as if prescribed by her favorite doctor. When she first started taking the medicine, she noticed that her urine turned greenish. It scared her at first, but she remembered that her had friend told her the urine would change colors and that this meant the infection was clearing. Anne knew it was not smart to just take someone's advice on an issue as serious as this without consulting with a professional. But she did notice that she wasn't going to the bathroom as frequently, and the pressure in her abdomen had gone away. And what a great feeling not to run to the bathroom every ten minutes!

Anne noticed, though, a persistent vaginal discharge that was foul and yellow in color. This scared her and made her question herself. She knew that she was a very clean person. She was always sure to pay special attention to her hygiene, and that had always been first and foremost to her. Anne started thinking about how her mother would always tease her about taking so many showers in one day. She said that she would melt away. Anne understood that all women had to be extra aware of maintaining their bodies, to take the finger test and make certain that things smelled kosher. Anne made sure her girls were at there best, not wanting the boys to shun them.

The lights and sirens went on in her head because between the bleeding, infection, and discharge, things were getting serious. The antibiotics had not taken away the discharge or the foul odor. She didn't have the pressure in her abdomen anymore, but that was the least of her concerns. She could smell herself. It was time to see the doctor! She knew if she didn't go to the doctor that this would overtake her and humiliate her if nothing else. Being around people every day would be embarrassing. Didn't matter how many times she went in the bathroom to make sure that she was clean. If you are sick, you are sick. Getting checked out was the only solution.

Anne was thinking they'd tell her she had some STD or other. She was so petrified that she was sweating bullets while waiting for them to call her name. She couldn't go to her regular OB-GYN out of embarrassment, so she found herself at the County Health Care Facility. When she walked in, she felt as if everyone in the building knew what she was there for. And if she'd only stare at them hard enough, she'd figure out why they were in there too. She saw teenage mothers strolling newborn babies, WIC mothers waiting in line for baby food, welfare recipients, and of course the patients already maligned with STDs or AIDS and other infectious diseases. She felt like she had reached the bottom of the barrel. She felt invaded because she was so out of place. Anne said to herself, "I'm not supposed to be here, so why am I here?" The nurse called her name then and asked Anne how many partners had she had and whether she practiced safe sex with these partners. With people running in and out of the office as they sat together, Anne's answers came in a barely audible whisper. There was no privacy at all. She kept thinking, "Who could I have gotten this from? I know I haven't been sleeping with no one else besides Curtis and Ty. I know Ty isn't out screwing anyone, and Curtis said he would tell me."

Anne was confused and getting more and more pissed off the more people who brushed past her to get to the examination room beyond where she sat. She told the nurse everything; she felt really scared now. She asked the nurse for an AIDS test. Anne knew she had to have something. She was resigned to curing it and getting it all over with and out in the open. While the nurse asked more questions, Anne's mind blanked out, and she began to shake uncontrollably. The nurse finally asked the question that made Anne feel like crawling under the medical bed and just die.

"Are you married?" the nurse asked.

Anne lowered her head and said meekly, "Yes."

Anne felt that the nurse had every right to condemn her for being unfaithful to her husband and now to have contracted a disease because of it. She had prepared herself for any news the doctor would give her. The urinalysis came back negative about possible pregnancy (Anne had had a tubule ligation and was not worried about being pregnant). It happened that a friend had gotten pregnant even with tubes tied, but Anne knew her body and was convinced pregnancy was the least of her troubles.

The doctor came in and introduced himself. He looked to be a native of Africa and was very attractive with a mass of wavy hair. He smelled good too, and Anne thought, "Damn, that's all I need is a very handsome doctor looking inside of me in my worst condition."

"Could you please go behind the curtains and take off your clothing from the waist down?"

Anne thought he would leave while she did so, but he stayed in the room with his back facing her, and she hurried, taking off her clothes

Flash Gordon fast. This was unheard of, a doctor staying in the room while you changed into the bottomless nightgown. Anyway, Anne was already at her humblest point and did everything the doctor and nurse asked her to do. She got up in the stirrups, and he examined her. He informed Anne of everything he was doing to make her feel comfortable. It didn't. She still felt like dying right there. It was an awful feeling, and she would never wish it on anyone. Finally he was done, and Anne was ready for the worst.

"Could you please get dressed, and I will be back," he said. Anne's mind wandered about the possibilities. What was she going to tell Curtis and Ty? She had to tell them both that they needed to get checked out. Convinced she had caught something, she wondered who in the hell Curtis had been sleeping with to get what he gave her. Her mind strayed to the darkest corners. "Yeah, Ty pretends to be so boring and tired that he's fucking some bitch and that's who gave me this shit."

Lost in her thoughts, she was startled when the doctor reentered the room. Anne looked at him in a melancholy mood. He looked at her and with his deep accent said that she had a vaginal bacteria caused by too much douching, deodorant soaps, tampons, and colored tissue. Kind of like a yeast infection but to the fifth power. He said it wasn't any form of STD, and with the medicine he prescribed, the symptoms would clear in a couple of days.

"Thank you Jesus," Anne said to herself over and over again.

He gave Anne a pamphlet to read and advised her on the use of condoms, saying some bodies can reject the injection of foreign objects, like penises. She wanted to laugh she was so relieved and overjoyed and looking forward to the sex she would still be having without condoms.

23
The Gym

After the night spent over at Curtis's house and the syphilis scare, Anne decided that she needed a break. She had never let him in on all the details, and until she knew what was going on with her own body, she had determined to distance herself from him. Curtis didn't know how to respond, but he knew that he had to try to move on. He had caused enough problems in her life and knew it wasn't fair to continue to ruin her marriage. But the only way he would be able to forget about Anne was to involve himself in someone else and quick. The longer he went home and lay in bed alone, the more tempted he would be to call Anne or, god forbid, Janice. And he knew that both of these women were to be off limits if he wanted his life on track. Curtis decided it was due time to put out some feelers.

He had seen her in the gym on several occasions, and other than a quick smile and a hello, he had never thought anything of it. She was a petite white woman with a pretty smile. Her complexion was dark from every day at the tanning booth, and she had a nice set of legs that along with her smile more and more attracted him. Her ass wasn't that amazing, but there weren't too many white girls who had junk in their trunk, so he could overlook it. Curtis could tell from her exercises, she was focused on building her gluteus. Not much of an ass man himself, he thought a nice ass couldn't hurt, but it didn't have to be Beyoncé ass to qualify. Curtis instead preferred the breasts. He had met several women with implants, and while he had nothing against them, the real ones were the ones he could call home.

Curtis had spoken to this new woman occasionally when their paths crossed on the gym floor. Every now and then there would be a comment made and a flirtatious glance, but hell, he knew when he came out of the locker room after a good workout with his biceps bulging, she couldn't help but stare. At the same time, this was normal gym protocol. That's why people came to the gym, to gawk and be gawked at. He never thought anything of it. Anne had long stopped coming to the gym with him, and they'd both had to admit finally that their relationship had become really too stressful.

Curtis had begun a new routine of leaving his cube and hitting the on-site gym for a fifteen-minute burnout, just to get Anne off his mind. He never thought he would ever get involved with anyone else at work, let alone a white woman. Curtis had nothing against them, but he had never been in a serious relationship with one.

Her name was Devan.

He was going to his car one day and saw Devan talking to a friend of his in the parking garage. The way they were together made him think they were dating. Curtis's mind now had two things on her. One, she liked black men, and two, he wasn't going to touch her. Curtis had a rule about the ex's of his buddies, which was don't touch 'em.

After seeing Devan with Chris, Curtis asked Devan about him. She informed Curtis that he was only a friend and that they never dated, but because he had made a special trip to their job site, she was obliged to spend time with him. The story confused Curtis, who tended to believe his eyes and his first instinct more than what other people told him. There was more going on with them. It was plain to see, but if she wasn't willing to admit it, he wouldn't push her.

Several weeks passed before Curtis saw Devan again. He had stopped going to the gym during his lunch break, and since that was the only place he normally saw Devan, she left his mind.

It was only when they were reintroduced that Curtis took Devan more seriously as a prospect for lover to be. Curtis had been appointed coordinator of an annual fundraising drive. Devan had signed up to take part, and this was how Curtis learned her name. All the times they had spoken to each other had been done without introduction.

When Devan entered the room, Curtis immediately felt some type of connection. He couldn't explain it, but he knew she felt it too. She sat up front in the seat closest to him, and he tried his best not to stare at her, but he couldn't keep his eyes off her. He had only seen her in real clothes a couple of times, but at that time he never noticed her because he was unaware of her preferences in men. Now it was a little different. Although he wasn't sure she dated black guys, he had a good idea she did. This would change the way he interacted with her. He was going to let her know that he was interested in her, he thought, and then the chips could fall where they may. Although he was still going back and forth with Anne about unfinished shit, he wanted someone he could call his own finally.

Curtis had volunteered to chair most of the meetings and organize the main event. During the meeting he informed all the participants what events they would be in, and he told Devan that they would work together just to get an idea of what she might be thinking. By agreeing, she gave Curtis the green light he'd waited and hoped for. Before Curtis excused everyone from the meeting, Devan raised her hand and said that she would assist in any way necessary. Curtis told her that everything was under control and that if he needed help he would let her know. Although he wanted to tell her that he would love her to help him, he could not because he had already recruited the assistance of another beautiful woman. Although Curtis didn't accept her offer, he was glad she had done so because this afforded him reason to call her, bogus or not. She was the last to leave when the meeting adjourned, and he felt that this would be the perfect time to introduce himself.

"By the way, my name is Curtis. It's nice to meet you officially."

Devan replied, "And I'm Devan. It's very nice to meet you."

"Damn, her voice was seductive and innocent," Curtis thought. "A curious mix."

They made small talk for a few minutes more before going back to their cubicles. Curtis decided he'd send her an e-mail to follow up and tell her how happy he was to have finally met her and that he would like to get to know her better. Before he'd had a chance to put his hands behind his head, lounged back in his chair, he'd received a reply from her letting him know he could call her whenever he wanted.

"Damn, damn, damn," Curtis thought.

Although their first contact was promising, Curtis decided not to call her a lot. He would call her from time to time, very casually, unaffectedly, and just to say hello. He was already in a relationship that he knew would be ending soon, so from that aspect, he was in no hurry to rush into another. He'd see her next at a kickoff party for the fundraiser.

24
Mind Made Up

B y day's end the day before the kickoff party, Curtis made two decisions that would affect this part of his life.

It started when he was on his way home one day and picked up a bottle of Grey Goose. He'd put the bottle in the backseat and pulled down the convertible top to see the lovely blue sky. It was the most terrific sunset he had seen all year. It was late November, although the weather was like late September. The sunset was somehow more beautiful than ever because of the slight change in the weather. The clouds were shaped like a handheld fan draped over a sky prettier than the bluest eyes he'd ever seen. The sun was going down, and it rested at the base of it all. It was as if God was trying to warn him of calm before the storm. It was all so spectacular and breathtaking; Curtis would never forget it as the last bright moment of this day. He deeply believed in the presence of signs. All over, one could see the signs.

Now all he could do was think about seeing Anne. She too had started going to the local jazz shows, and although they had not talked much, he understood from the route to avoid each other, not all was over. Eclipsed in the beautiful sunset, he half wished she were there to share it with him. He wanted her to feel the emotions that were running through his body and soul.

He wanted to lay on his horn or just toot a little bit though it would not help much the heavy flow of traffic at rush hour. A young woman's eyes, he noticed, were piercing through him from her rear-view mirror. Curtis didn't know why she continued to stare, but the more she did, the more he had a strange feeling about her intense stare. This seem to be another one of those signs that this night would be one to remember.

He'd had plans for the night, and nothing was going to interfere. He got home from work around six thirty, put a couple of hot dogs on his George Foreman, and threw some Ramen noodles on the stove. Yes, it was budget food, but he knew his stomach could not be on empty for all the drinking that was to come. The weather was finally cool enough to bring out a shirt he had bought on sale at the beginning of the summer. It was a baby blue Polo sport shirt with long sleeves that made him look ten years younger. Curtis would wear the same jeans he had worn to work that day and his Timberlands. Dressing after a shower, he fixed himself a drink, tuning his flat screen to the smooth R&B station. He couldn't wait to see Anne, he realized.

Curtis arrived about twenty minutes early. The band hadn't started, and the stage was still empty. He went to his usual seat and waited. He poured himself another drink from his private stash he had managed to sneak inside. Before he could finish his drink, the band began to play. The lead singer was a pretty blonde with a voice that just pierced through his soul. She reminded him of Mary J. Blige when she'd go blonde. But it was her sax player that brought it home.

Curtis had sat through a couple of songs before any of his friends began to appear. He had been coming here for over five years, and the faces remained the same. Some would come rain or shine. Anne had just started coming last year. She hated that Curtis had so many other friends there because she never had his full attention, but she seemed to enjoy herself. After an hour and a half went by, Curtis thought he was going to spend the night alone. No Anne and no signs of anybody else. Then at eight thirty, Kenny showed up.

Kenny and he shared their favorite spot. He was happy to see Kenny finally. The Goose was working, and Curtis was getting a little upset because Anne still had not shown up. Of course, she had made promises before that she would break, but for whatever reason, perhaps out of his loneliness, he felt this was the last straw. Curtis and Kenny had a chance to catch up, having not seen each other in a few months. Curtis reminded him of the Rick James CD that he wanted back. Another hour had passed when Curtis's phone rang. His coworkers were calling to see where he was sitting.

"On the east side of the band with a friend of mine, the same place I sit every time I come," Curtis explained.

Curtis was a little short because he hadn't heard from Anne all this time, and he'd really thought that was her calling. As they headed in his direction, Curtis told Kenny that they would be accompanied by a few women from his job, that they were all single, and if he played his cards right, he might get lucky.

He gave Curtis a high five and said, "Bring on the hoes, dog."

Kenny took up immediately with Lauren, a middle-aged white woman with long curly hair, a thin build, dark complexion. She was not drop dead but pretty but she looked good for her age. Curtis had already told them that Anne would be there. After they all were talking for about fifteen minutes, Lauren asked about Anne. By now, Curtis figured that she would not be joining them, so he got a little sarcastic and said, "I don't believe she is coming. Hell, it must be past her bedtime."

As soon as he said it, somebody shouted, "There's Anne!"

As Curtis glanced over and found her making her way to him through the crowd, he wanted to punch himself over the way she was looking. She was wearing a tiger print tight blouse with a knee length skirt and a pair of boots. Her hair was going off as well. She glanced back at Curtis with those eyes that made him melt.

Curtis had to figure out a way to get her away from all these people. She had already explained to him that she wanted to be alone with him tonight, and if he had known for sure that she was coming, he would have left the crowd behind. As she greeted everyone else, he stood and gave her a hug and whispered in her ear.

"Hey we need to excuse ourselves to the restroom," Curtis said.

She understood exactly what he meant. They always had this chemistry. And the practice of coding their conversations had never concealed each other's thoughts. After about five minutes, Curtis said that he was going to the restroom, and she was right on cue.

"I will walk with you," she said.

It was impossible to keep their hands off each other. Curtis was walking in front of Anne, and she held him from behind as if they were truly a couple. He knew they were going to have the time of their lives that night.

Curtis told her he would go back to their circle and find a way to excuse himself from the rest of their friends and that she should do the same. He was thinking they could meet up across the street. But Anne said, "No, I'm not going back there. I just want to spend the night with you."

Curtis said, "Fine, but at least, let's say good-bye."

"You go if you want to, but I'm not going back over there," Anne insisted.

"I don't understand why we couldn't go back and leave after a couple of minutes," he said. "Shit, we're going to be together the rest of the night," Curtis said. As he spoke, the Goose seemed to speak back to him. "So what's really going on, Anne? Is there a reason you can't walk back over with me?"

. He probably thought she had met someone before she ran across him, and that's what had made her so late. Curtis didn't know what was going on, but Anne was acting different. She was cheating on both him and Ty! The Grey Goose Curtis was drinking had him thinking irrationally. Wasn't it hard enough dealing with her marriage? Now he had something else to wonder about? Curtis convinced himself that the true reason she had been late and had not called was that she was seeing somebody else on the side. Somebody she must be trying to get to. This was his punishment, wasn't it? Curtis thought.

He looked at her and said, "Fuck it, do what ever your ass wants to do."

He walked off. Anne looked at Curtis in astonishment. She didn't know what had gotten into him. As he walked away from Anne, he couldn't believe that she might have been trying to meet with someone else there. It was as if someone had taken his heart out of his chest and ripped it in half. He knew that he was in love with Anne, but to what extent and to what degree, he had never known until then. As he walked off, he wanted to cry. He could already envision them in bed screwing each other's brains out.

Curtis ran into a friend of his whom he had not seen in a long time. They had never been sexually involved, but they were close to it at one time. He stopped, hugged her, and asked her how she had been doing; unaware that Anne was following him. The girl asked Curtis about his next trip to New York, said she wanted to join him. He told her he would call her.

"Are you here alone tonight?" Curtis asked her.

"Yes," she said. "Why?"

"Just wondering," Curtis answered.

The girl said she wished that she had taken Curtis up on the room-mate proposal he had made last year. "I didn't think it would be a good idea for us to be around each other so much," the girl said sheepishly.

"Well, it's still a possibility," Curtis offered. He was pissed off at Anne. After he somewhat flirted with this girl, Anne brushed past him heading back to their friends. Curtis had just realized that Anne had heard the entire conversation. He broke up the conversation with the girl to catch up with Anne. By the time he got there, she had gone, and everyone else was preparing to leave. Curtis tried to call Anne on the phone. The phone rang several times, and then her answering machine came on. Now he was fuming. Now he wanted to kick her ass.

"Why am I getting so mad?" Curtis asked himself.

He tried to calm down, but every time he thought about her, he was wound up again. He tried to call her again. The phone rang two times, and she answered, "May I help you?"

"What the fuck do you mean may I help you? You can't talk to me?" Curtis said.

"I don't want to talk," Anne said and hung up.

"Okay, fuck it then. I'm done with this shit," Curtis said to himself. "I can't believe this woman got me talking to myself."

He called her ass again. This time, she didn't pick up. He called her four more times, and she never picked up her phone. He just knew now that she was with someone else. Curtis eventually made it home and calmed himself. This night didn't go as planned, and he started thinking. The Grey Goose he was drinking didn't make matters any better. He and Grace had never gotten a divorce, and it always haunted him that he hadn't let her go completely. He knew that he should still be home with his family. With Grace. He decided that he would call her and finally release her. He called his wife and told her that he wanted a divorce. He was tired of that shit too. Although Grace never troubled Curtis, there was a lot of corresponding with her. He didn't know how she would take what he was going to say, but she didn't seem to care one way or the other anymore. Her nonchalant attitude reignited Curtis. He was pissed all over again. He was hoping that she would argue about him calling so late. Say something to trigger a response. But she didn't. She didn't seem to care anymore. When Curtis hung up with Grace, he realized that he was still in love with her, but was trying to find other love in all the wrong places. Grace was supposed to cry, yell, and curse, something to make him think. She did neither; she just calmly said ok and hung up the phone.

Curtis picked up the phone again and called Anne. She answered, "HELLO."

"No, don't answer that motherfucker now. Shit, I want to leave a message," Curtis hollered.

Anne hung up then, and Curtis called right back. When her answering machine came on, he said, "I'm not sure who your ass was trying to get to tonight, but I hope you enjoyed yourself. I thought that we would really enjoy our night together, but I guess you had another option. Well, I cannot do this shit anymore. It is starting to get too difficult. I really enjoyed the time we have spent together. I hope we can remain friends." There was sarcasm in his last line. He thought she would really appreciate that bit.

Curtis's phone rang immediately, and he didn't answer. She left a message. "I don't know why you think I was trying to be with someone else. You know I wanted to be with you tonight. I love you, and you know this. This is what I mean by I already have strikes against me. You are always going to judge me no matter the evidence."

Curtis turned off the light and lay down in the bed. A tear rolled down his cheek. He thought that she was right, and there was not a damned thing he could do about it.

25

Anne Ends It

I t had been a while since Curtis and Anne had been together. Christmas had come and gone, and Curtis was feeling the emptiness of the holidays. He had spent another night out alone. Getting up this morning was hard to do. As Curtis looked around his bedroom, he could see the reminiscence of a long night out, that is, a long night out without getting lucky. The beer that he had snuck out of the club was sitting in a pathetically condensed puddle of water. His wallet had toppled his entire collection of cologne bottles as though he had thrown it there from the doorway. One of his shoes was still on his foot, while the other was in the doorway. He must have tried to remove his shirt because all of the buttons were undone except for one. He must have gotten tired of unbuttoning. His pants were lying across the chair at the computer desk inside out, and all of a sudden he realized that he had such a headache that he wished he could take his head off into his lap to massage it.

Reality had just hit Curtis—he'd just spent New Year's Eve at a local club, drunk as hell to come home alone like some pitiful old man.

As he mustered up the strength to come to his feet, he stumbled into the kitchen to look for the Tylenol bottle he had reserved for just these occasions. He couldn't remember making it home last night at all. He knew that he shouldn't have been driving, but he had gone to the club alone, so there was no designated driver.

"Just be thankful you're in one piece," he told himself.

After he swallowed the tablets, he headed straight for the fridge. The squeak of the refrigerator door pierced his skull and intensified the throbbing. He needed some type of liquid. Curtis's mouth was dry and sticky, and there had to be something that would help to moisten his lips. He found a can of Coke that had been in there for about a week and tasted like flat sugar. He gulped it in one swift motion and started looking for something else.

Curtis's refrigerator was the bachelor's model. There were three or four take-out boxes, some loose ketchup and mustard packets, a box of just add water pancake mix, half of a ham that his mom had given him on Christmas day along with eight beers. Curtis grabbed one of the beers, opened it, and downed it in about sixty seconds. His dad had always told him the best thing for a hangover is a cold beer. He was going to test all sorts of old wisdom today.

As he turned the can up into the air, Curtis said, "Happy New Year to me." He grabbed another beer and stumbled back into the room. As long as he could remember, he had never spent New Year's Eve alone. Even if he didn't get lucky, he still usually had a good time. Curtis had always spent the night home with Grace, sipping on champagne and watching the ball drop. He had been content to stay at home with her. It seems that he always thought about his time with Grace every time he faced diversity. It seemed so much a distant nearness. Too far to touch and too close to forget. He felt like shit now and wanted to drink all over again.

Curtis thought, "I'm seeing someone's else's wife, and although I sort of like being able to send her home on those nights I don't want to be bothered, on the days I really need someone, she has to spend those moments with her family."

He hadn't seen Anne much since the night at the jazz show and knew that it was really over between them. "This is a new year. I have to do things differently this year. I have to find someone who's mine, who will be for me," he said, "if possible," he added.

Curtis went over to the mirror where the bottles were overturned. "How did I get here in the first place? I don't know who the hell I am anymore. It seems like it was only yesterday when I was working on the light fixtures in my house."

Curtis had done all of the home renovations himself, even the decorations. He was the decorator and the fix-it man. Grace would put her two cents in about some of the décor, but Curtis was the one with flair for that sort of thing. He remembered when they had bought the house. It was the last place they looked at. They had seen so many houses in the month of looking, and then, at the last minute, there it was; it was in their budget and in the area they wanted to live. Curtis had told the broker that this was the last day they were looking, that if they didn't find something, they'd wait and try it some other time.

The realtor had informed Curtis that he had one more house he wanted him to see. He said that the house needed a little TLC but had a lot of character, and the owners were motivated to sell. All that broker mumbo jumbo Curtis had heard a thousand times. But when Curtis and Grace arrived at the house, he was floored. He remembered he and Grace just looking at each other, looking at the house, and then looking back at each other.

Their first impression was the house was small. Everything including the front door was very old. It was missing a hinge or two. The broker explained that the house had been sitting for a few months, that some of the kids from the neighborhood had been caught in there having a party.

Curtis was reminded of the beer bottles they had seen in the trash bin as they approached the house. Once inside, Curtis and Grace felt like the house seemed to go on forever. He couldn't believe how spacious after the threshold. Every room was larger than the norm. The walls were a little banged up, but nothing a couple of sheets of drywall and paint couldn't fix.

The foyer led them into a spacious sunken living room with the nastiest carpet Curtis had ever seen. It was as if someone had been using the area as a bathroom stall. Wherever there was carpeting, the odor of dog urine prevailed.

Grace ran out of the house. Curtis looked at the realtor and told him that they were done, and they would try again in about a month. He insisted that they finish looking at the rest of the house. He led them back into the house and up to the bedrooms on the south wing. Each room was spacious. Even the bathroom was sizable. All the cabinets and fixtures needed replacing, but the house had been well built and remained structurally sound. Curtis went on to the master bedroom, the room that required least work.

The master bath had new tile, new fixtures, and an awesome Jacuzzi that still looked clean. The more Curtis saw, the more the house grew on him. They completed the tour and went out through the backdoor. In the yard, three fruit trees needed trimming and the pool needed serious maintenance and cleaning. The size of the pool reduced the backyard and the amount of yard work he'd have to do. They left by a rusted gate.

Grace was sitting in the car with the AC on, looking at Curtis as if he were crazy to think it.

As Curtis sat there reminiscing about the day he and Grace decided on that house a smile flickered across Curtis's face and disappeared as soon as it had appeared. The memory left as quick as it came and Curtis was back in his house, a cold beer in his hand, checking e-mails on New Year's Day, just to see if he'd get just one holiday wish.

The only e-mail Curtis was from Anne. She was always a thoughtful person. He was expecting a love letter—that's right, a lovely New Year's love letter. Something was off though. The subject line was the generic type. A strange feeling came over him even before he read:

Happy New Year's...Hope all is well with you. I am doing great! I felt the need to write instead of call because I'm a chicken. Well, I wanted to get out everything that's on my mind before I change my mind. You may or may not have noticed calls on your work phone at weird hours. Well, Ty noticed calls to Drocoa on his phone bill and c'd the number. He asked me who it was, and I said Arthur, so he called the number and gave me the phone and asked me whose voice that was, and I said Arthur's. I am so tired of telling lies that it's consuming me. So if you see unfamiliar numbers on your phone, it may be him calling. Anyway, I said all of that to say this. I love you dearly, and you know that already, but I have to be an honest woman and be true and faithful or else leave Ty and be with you. I don't want to mess up your life with uncertainties, so I'm going to give it another try with Ty. If it doesn't work, I can honestly say that I have tried, and I gave it my all with no outside interference. I know you heard me say this numerous times before, and you have tried to respect my wishes, so I'm asking again to respect my wishes. I'm not going to call you anymore, and please don't call me. I need to end all ties I have with you because that's the only way I can concentrate on my marriage. You will always be in my heart till the day I take my last breath. You stood by me in all ways and I THANK YOU FOR EVERYTHING! I just need to be true to myself, stop misleading myself and going around thinking of myself as a liar. The truth is I love my husband, and the other truth is I love you. You've brought me joy that I haven't had in a long time. Reality is though, I'm married and not single. P.S. In no way is this your fault if you are wondering it. I needed to do this for my family and for myself. It's always hard loving two people at the same time. Take care,

Love always,

Anne

There. Now it was done. She had finally broken it off with him, and although they had gone down this road before, this time would be different. It was over, and he knew it. Curtis tried to be a man about it, but after the first tear dropped, he couldn't stop the one that followed. He was now truly alone, and with a fortieth birthday on the horizon.

26

A Day in Court

S oon after the new year started, Curtis received a knock on the door one day.

"Are you Curtis Caldwell?" the guy at the door asked.

"Yes, how can I help you?" Curtis asked.

"Could you please sign for these papers?"

It had finally happened. Curtis was being served with divorce papers. This gave him a queasy feeling in the pits of his abdomen. He knew he had called Grace that night and asked for a divorce, but he didn't realize it would be so soon. He realized that it had been a couple of years since the separation, and it was time. Grace had waited patiently for his return, which never happened. After the night she received the phone call, she was tired of trying to get Curtis to come home and decided to give him what he asked for.

The date was set for a month from the date he got the visit. It seemed to come so quickly. Curtis was unsure what to wear since he had never attending this type of hearing before. He just wore a button down shirt and a pair of slacks. He felt that would be appropriate. He and Grace arrived at the same time. She wore a skirt that stopped right above her knees and a pair of black pumps. Grace had always had the prettiest legs Curtis had ever seen. This was one of the features that attracted him to her. Her top was conservative, but it accented her perfect body. As they approached the elevator, Curtis complimented her on how beautiful she was, and she just smiled as if to say thanks. Grace and Curtis had been cordial with each other since the separation and never argued after that day at his friend's house. The elevator ride seemed to go on forever, and it was very awkward. Curtis tried small talk, but it didn't work. He was about to finalize a part of his life he never thought would ever end. He never fell out of love with Grace; he just made a bad mistake that he couldn't live with. He knew that deep down he really didn't want to let his marriage go, but he couldn't go on seeing the hurt he had caused Grace. He thought the only option they had was divorce.

Once they entered the General Master's office, they were seated on opposite side of the room. They assumed that all these hearings weren't pleasant, hence the separation. As the lady in charge started stating the clauses in the decree, Curtis and Grace started to communicate with each other, and the young lady advised them both not to speak to one another. Curtis had never been told that he could not talk to his wife, and he had gotten a little upset. The reality of divorce was starting to sink in. Once they left this room, the only connection they would share would be the children. This saddened Curtis more than anything he had ever been associated with up to this point in his life, but nevertheless, he signed the papers as well as Grace. Both of them had the opportunity to stop it, but didn't. It was over.

Curtis didn't ride down the elevator with her, but decided to take the stairs. As he reached the bottom of the last staircase, he broke down to his knees and started crying. He couldn't believe that the woman he married for sickness and health, good or bad, forever to death, was no longer his wife. How could I be so stupid? he kept thinking. After a few minutes, a baliff entered the stairwell and asked Curtis if he was okay. There had been several instances where people have actually attempted to hurt themselves after divorce hearings, and they were monitoring

Curtis the entire time. He gathered his composure and he assured the officer that he was okay, picked up his pride and exited the building. When Curtis pulled into his driveway, he couldn't remember the ride home and was totally exhausted. He lay down in bed and didn't awake until the next day.

27

Curtis Turns Forty

C urtis couldn't believe he was dancing on top of the bar with two of the prettiest girls in the club. They wore tight black pants and pink half shirts, and there they were, dancing his night away with him. He was sure that their perfect abs contributed to the kinds of moves these girls were making. As he danced his life away, trying to keep up with them, he thought, "How did I get here?"

It was his first birthday celebration without family. Since he had been married, all his parties had always been the same. They would either have dinner at his mother's or have a few people over to the house for a cookout. Nothing wrong with those parties, but this was his fortieth after all, and there was no more family. So he would have to make it a night to remember.

The only other birthday that had been significant in Curtis's memory was his sixteenth. This was the first birthday party that he had really enjoyed. He had planned all of it and invited everyone he knew, friend or enemy. He had packed up his mother's garage wall to wall with so many faces; she had talked about it for years. Curtis was the talk of the town for about two months because of that party. He could remember it being the first time he had a chance to really dance with his girlfriend. They weren't old enough to go to clubs, and they never had any other places to go and dance.

They seemed to dance forever that night. They seemed to be made for each other that night. She was one of the finest girls in school, and Curtis was proud to be dancing with her. His mother was working that night, and she left his father to supervise, and he seemed to be having as much fun as anybody else.

All the kids were all drinking beer and doing all the things that high school kids shouldn't be doing. After a few beers, Curtis asked his girlfriend to come into the house to get away from the noise to talk. Although they had never had sex, they always had a good time when they were alone. She would get him so turned on that he would always go home with the blue balls.

When they got into the house, he took her to his room. They started kissing and touching as they always did. Curtis told her that he really wanted to be with her sexually and that this would be a perfect birthday gift. She agreed, and they made love for a stretch that seemed like hours. This really put a perfect end on a day that had already been perfect.

Now Curtis found himself dancing on a bar with people he really didn't know. Sure, they all worked together, but he would never feel that he really knew them. Still, it was turning out to be more fun than his sixteenth. Curtis had invited several friends from previous jobs. Everybody was getting along fine. It was one big party, and he was the center of attention. As the night went on, everyone started getting more and more intoxicated, and Curtis's boss started really flirting with him. They had always very innocently flirted at other outings, but for some reason, tonight took on a whole new meaning. As they danced together, her moves became more and more suggestive, and the more they danced the more he wanted to screw her.

Curtis was still getting over his relationship with Anne and the divorce. He hadn't been with anyone since. Curtis really tried his best to restrain himself, but between the margaritas and the proximity of her moves, he longed to get closer and closer to her. They found themselves dirty dancing on the floor, and his other coworkers had to be asking themselves what in the hell was going on. They had never openly flirted, and he didn't care—this was his birthday. He just hoped everybody was drunk enough never to remember. They finally broke apart, but she'd managed to get his keys, so before the night was over, he knew he would have to catch up to her. The night was coming to an end, and everyone was leaving, his boss and some others decided they'd find another club and drink some more. The heat between Curtis and his boss had gotten unbearable. As they arrived at the other club, Curtis and Delores picked up where they left off. They danced until they each were sweating profusely.

Before he knew it, the lights of the club went on. The others had gone on ahead of them. Curtis decided that his boss was too drunk to take her car. They both had been drinking and probably should have taken a cab, but he decided that they should take his car. On the way to her place, they stopped for a bite to eat, and she started complaining about how badly her feet hurt.

Curtis joked that he would rub them for her. And before he could tell her that he was only kidding, she had her feet in his lap as though all night she had been waiting for him to make a real pass. Curtis looked into her eyes as he rubbed and tickled her feet. They left the drive-through, and Curtis was now driving a little faster than he was before. He didn't want these feelings to go away. They arrived at her house where Curtis sat on the floor to finish his food.

She came over to him and put her feet in his hands again, and he started messaging them, but this time a little more seductively. He then began to rub her calves, working up to her thighs until he'd made his way to the edge of her panties. Curtis could feel the beginnings of her pelvic thrust and gyrations. She was overdue for a little TLC. This also started a reaction in him that only happens when he was about to get laid. He reached up, pulled up her dress, and kissed the lining of her underwear, and she moaned softly, grabbed the back of his head, and tried to direct it to the middle of her legs.

Curtis hadn't planned on letting things progress quite this way, but before he could stop, that Hennessy he was drinking at the club pushed him to forge ahead and give her what she wanted. She probably felt like a queen to have a brother down there getting ready to give her an experience she would have never expected since brothers are not known for oral sex. Little did she know, he was well versed and adept at pleasing.

Delores was in her midforties and had been married to one guy since she was eighteen. She did everything for her husband that a wife could possibly do except have children. Of course, he wanted those kids she couldn't have, so there was always that obstacle. Someday, he'd leave her and let her die a statistic. As far as Curtis could tell, she had never dated a black man, but she had been attracted to Curtis since the first interview.

At work, they were professionals. There had been neither time nor room for anything else, but tonight, tonight was a different matter. Tonight, Delores could satisfy her curiosity, quench her thirst. She had always heard that a black man in bed was an intense man with stamina, speed, and agility. Several of her white friends had dated black guys before, and they all had pretty much the same story. It would be her turn to see if she went black. Would she be tempted not to go back?

So far Curtis was exceeding expectations with the foot rub. She hadn't been told nor had she expected romance, and that was not to mention the kiss. The kiss was perfect. He gave her just enough tongue, and she returned the favor. What he had in store though was exceptional. She couldn't believe his next move. Curtis, having decided that he would tease her before he took the plunge, rubbed his tongue up and down the outside of her designer underwear until he located her clitoris. Curtis started messaging it with his tongue, and her hips started to move uncontrollably. He reached around and grabbed her ass to slow her down a little, and at the same time, his finger followed the string that went along the crack of her ass and slowly rubbed his fingers around the edge of her asshole. She finally got into the rhythm that he was looking for. She wanted Curtis to fill every orifice she had though little did she know her wishes were about to come true. She was on the verge of having her first orgasm, and at this time he realized she was a multiorgasmic woman. Wait though. He wasn't ready for her to come just yet.

Curtis raised his head and saw her eyes roll. She was already feeling it. She was about to come. He reached up then and put his finger in her mouth, and she sucked on it as if it was a baby's bottle. He wanted to know the intensity of her orgasm. If she stopped sucking on that finger, he knew her orgasm would be wild and intense. If nothing else, Curtis had learned one thing about women: when she is having a good orgasm, she can't do much else.

As he noticed Delores's rhythm change and watched her climbing to that peak, still using his finger as a pacifier, he told himself it was going to be one long night. She would have several orgasms, and he would have to go into his bag of tricks to take her mind off everything else. Before long she was out of those T-backs, and Curtis was giving her the complete package. He had never given this to any other woman on the first date, but for some reason, after weighing all the options, he thought it would be in his best interest to make her remember the night. Curtis had explored the walls of her vagina with his tongue and even went as far as teasing the other hole she had down there. She had already had two orgasms before he'd had a chance to stick his penis in her.

Delores couldn't believe the feelings that were going through her mind and body at the time. She had experienced only a couple of other guys after her divorce. But this Curtis! This Curtis was definitely far superior, and she hadn't even experienced dick yet. Finally Curtis decided it was time for him to get his. As he penetrated the walls of her womanhood, she let out this quiet moan. Quiet enough to cause Curtis to have the quickest orgasm of his life. He couldn't believe that this woman had made him come this quick.

Curtis had always been multiorgasmic as well; this was one feature that he had always been proud of. Delores felt Curtis come inside her, and now it all made sense. He was so good at oral sex because his sex game was lacking. Although he was well endowed, well endowed doesn't matter if you can't stay erect.

He may have come, but he never stopped humping her. He stayed inside of her, and it seemed that his dick actually got harder after that first orgasm. She had never experienced anything like this before. The second one took over an hour to surface, but when it finally came, he could not believe how intense it was. Curtis had gotten what he was looking for. After the second orgasm, he figured it was time he put her ass to sleep. He rolled over on his back, and she followed as if he were leading her in a waltz.

Curtis reached around her ass, put his finger inside, and messaged the membrane between the inside of both of her holes, slowing his rhythm. He made sure his head was propped up just enough to put her nipples in his mouth. Being the mature woman she was, she only needed a little time before she got her groove on. He was patient and waited. All of a sudden he felt her grinding in a repeated motion. It was her time. Although she had come a couple of times already, she still had one intense orgasm that had not yet been discovered. She started grinding harder and harder; it was only a matter of time. Curtis took his other hand that was behind her head and maneuvered his finger into her mouth. He now occupied every hole in her body. She never started to suck on it; she was concentrating on that orgasm.

He thought, "Why do I do this to women?"

She let out a loud shriek and went motionless. Her body fell on top of his, and he put his arms around her and asked if she was okay.

She responded, "Wonderful." So he held her until she fell asleep.

28
Not in the Office

◧◨

T he next day at work was awkward for the first half of the day. Each time they talked, they did so without daring to look each other in the eye. Hell, this was his supervisor. What in the hell made them do the shit they did? They had to talk about what happened, but there was no way that they could do it during the workday. As days went by without either one mentioning what had happened on the night of Curtis's birthday, he thought perhaps it would never be discussed.

A few weeks later, there was another outing that they both attended. After a few drinks, they started dancing, taking up the same flame of the first night together. Once the lovemaking was over, they talked. They both admitted to enjoying time together, knowing it couldn't go much farther. After the talk, seeing her at work wasn't all that bad anymore. It was awkward before because neither one of them knew what the other was looking for. Defining their relationship made everything easier.

One night they both had to work late, and Delores came to Curtis's office to see how long he would be working. When he turned around in his chair, he realized that she was standing in his doorway with her shirt buttoned halfway down. She had on that same skirt from the first time he saw her and those four-inch pumps that made her legs look a mile long.

"How long are you working tonight, Curtis?" she asked.

"Oh, I'm not sure, probably another hour or so. I have to finish this report that you asked me to have on your desk tomorrow."

"You need to stop working so hard and take a break sometime," Delores said as she walked in his direction.

Curtis thought that if she got too close to him he would take her right there in his office. He had never had sex with her at work though he had fantasized. Everyone was gone, and he'd already concluded from his first glance at her that it wouldn't take much work to be inside of her, in her "catch me, hunch me" dress. Delores, meanwhile, had already made up her mind that she was going to fuck Curtis right there as he sat in his chair. She approached Curtis and sat in his lap. She stared into the computer screen.

"How are the projections going?" she asked.

Curtis reached around her and used his mouse to put the cursor on the spreadsheet he was working on. "As far as I can see, we are about a half million under budget, and I haven't added in all the variables yet. If I had to give you a preliminary report, we are looking real good," Curtis said as his dick started to react to her sitting on him.

Delores felt Curtis's penis rise, and she started to rotate her ass in a circular motion. Curtis reached around and put his hand into her shirt and realized that she had already removed her bra. He started massaging her nipple, which had already become erect. He used the other hand to finish unbuttoning her blouse. By the time Curtis had her blouse unbuttoned, he was fully erect, and she was grinding on his dick. Curtis grabbed both of her breasts and returned the grinding motions. Delores reached down and pulled up her skirt to show him that she wasn't wearing any panties. Curtis lowered his hand and started to massage Delores's clit, and the moistness from her almost drove him to orgasm. From the moan Delores let out, he could tell she had already reached one climax. Curtis did not want to come in his pants, so he lifted Delores slightly and unzipped his pants. He had gotten so hard. By the time he'd finished with the zipper, his penis had pushed through the slit in his underwear and popped out of its den. Curtis slowly lowered Delores onto his penis, and as it entered her body, she lost her breath. His penis had traveled deep inside her. It took her a few seconds to get used to the presence of his dick inside of her; no one had ever filled her like Curtis.

"Oh shit," she yelled out. When Curtis rose to meet her now soaked vagina, Delores put her hand on Curtis's thigh to control how much of his manhood was being inserted inside of her. Curtis started going up and down, in and out, at a slower and slower pace. Delores reached her second orgasm.

Curtis thighs, by now, had gotten so slippery from her moistness that her hand would slip from time to time, which caused his penis to go deeper than she wanted. She couldn't believe how good it felt. Curtis rose from his chair then and bent Delores over his desk. He was now enacting one of his all time fantasies. Delores's arms were spread across his desk. Her ass was in the perfect position, and Curtis laid pipe in her until he exploded with sheer fulfillment.

Curtis sat back down in his chair from complete exhaustion. Delores turned over and rested on his desk spread eagle. Curtis looked over at her and could see that her vagina was still just as pretty as it was when he'd seen it that first night. He rolled his chair around in front of Delores and ran his fingers across her abdomen. Her clitoris was standing in the position of attention. He could help himself. He licked his lips and put her clit between them while he played with it on his tongue. Delores jumped at the touch of Curtis's tongue, still sensitive from her last orgasm. Curtis held on with his lips for few seconds until he could feel her pelvis start to move again. He started to lick on her clit again as she grabbed the back of Curtis's head and pulled it in close. He reached up, pinched her nipples lightly, and stuck his middle finger in Delores's ass with his thumb in her vagina. Delores opened her legs as wide as she could before losing her ability to control her motions. She couldn't believe the feelings going through her body; she actually shed a tear or two. By the time she reached her fourth orgasm, she was completely overwhelmed. Curtis inserted his penis one more time and told her that this wouldn't take long. Within two minutes Curtis had reached his orgasm. He sat back down in the chair, breathing as if he had run a marathon. Delores summoned all the strength she had and got dressed.

"That report is due next week," she said. "Now, go home and get some rest. Take tomorrow off, if you'd like. You deserve it anyway." Delores walked out of Curtis's office and thought that she couldn't go on doing this, that she'd get too used to it, and it'd ultimately be more trouble than it was worth.

After the nights socializing with coworkers, no one would have suspected they were screwing each other's brains apart. The love affair with Delores was as brief as it was necessary, for both of them. She had been recently divorced, and Curtis was going through his own. They had found each other at the right time. The affair never interfered with their work relationship thanks to her discretion and maturity.

29
Kick-Off Party

T
wo months had passed, and Curtis hadn't seen Anne at all. She had found a way to dodge him at work, and he, for his part, had no intention of tracking her down. The last thing he wanted to do was go against her wishes. It was okay that they had stopped seeing each other. He had gotten tired of sneaking around with her only to go home alone. Although the times they spent together were magical, they both knew from the beginning that it wasn't going to last forever. If they had met twenty years ago, maybe things would have been better, or maybe they would be in the same predicament they were now. Who really ever knows? But Curtis was determined to forget about her, and he knew just how to do it.

The night of the big kick-off party for the event that Curtis was in charge of would be the night to leave that part of his life behind. Curtis hadn't seen Devan around the workplace, but he knew she would show up at the party. He had kept in touch with all the participants to give them updates as the date approached for the big event. Devan was one of the participants who always replied to his e-mails, and she would always say something to make Curtis smile. Her e-mails were flirtatious without seeming unprofessional. Devan had come on as the administrative assistant to the company's CEO. She was a sharp young lady who undeniably had her shit together. The only thing Devan was lacking, which many career women can be said to be lacking, seemed to be the man of her dreams with whom she could share her life and success. She lived in a townhouse condo with her daughter surrounded by all of the material comforts. She had chosen the father of her daughter for his tall, dark, and handsome features. Knowing that he could be a real asshole, she had chosen him for his genes above all else.

After her little girl was born, she never heard from him again. He was too fine, too structurally perfect, and too full of himself. It didn't take long for Devan to notice. She never told him that she was pregnant, and since he left town shortly after their brief encounter, she didn't feel compelled to tell him. She accepted the fact that she would raise her daughter alone or at least until she found the guy who would put a ring on her finger.

She had seen Curtis around work and knew that he was a nice guy. She also knew that he was married, so she had never really given him a second thought. Only at an office, news spreads like fleas, and the news of Curtis's breakup with Grace quickly spread. Though the details remained unknown, everybody seemed to know it had something to do with Janice. Janice and Curtis might have walled themselves up behind curtains, but nobody seemed to be fooled.

Devan had also noticed Curtis's friendship with Anne. Anne was married though, so Devan did not suspect anything more than friendship between them. It wasn't her business anyway. She wasn't even really interested. Curtis was vulnerable, fresh from a long-term relationship. She didn't want the burden of such baggage. Their e-mails were friendly. He was a nice guy after all, Devan thought.

Devan brought her girlfriend with her to the kickoff party. Devan's tan was deep and rosy brown, and her blue shirt brought out her ocean blue eyes. Devan noticed Curtis and went over to speak and she introduced her friend.

"Hi, Curtis, how are you?" she said.

Curtis turned, seeming surprised to see her suddenly standing there. "Oh, hi, Devan, how are you?"

"I'm good," she replied. "This is Amber, a good friend of mine."

Curtis reached out and shook Amber's hand, barely glancing at her. He was fixated on Devan; he had never seen her like this before, and he couldn't take his eyes off her. "You look very nice tonight, Devan," Curtis said.

"Thanks, you look pretty handsome yourself."

After a few minutes, Curtis excused himself to go pick up the shirts for the team. The young lady assisting him would only be there for a short time because she was married and had to get home. She informed Curtis that he had better take advantage of her while she was there.

For a brief moment, Curtis thought that she might be flirting with him, but he realized he was thinking with his other end and getting to be really full of himself now because she was happily married. Still fine as hell though, he thought watching her move. She was out of his reach, but she made for a good fantasy.

Once the shirts had been issued, his fine assistant left and told Curtis that she would see him tomorrow at the event.

"Don't stay out all night," she said.

He laughed and said he wasn't going to do anything that she wouldn't do. As she walked away, Curtis watched her ass go. What a nice body she had, he thought. He couldn't wait to see her again at the beach. All of a sudden his concentration was broken; Devan had walked in the path of the ass he was following out of the door.

"Damn," Devan said. "You might as well walk her to her car."

Curtis looked at Devan and smiled. "I did offer, but she assured me that she was okay, that her husband was outside waiting for her."

"Then you know it's not good to stare at another man's wife."

"Well, if you hadn't disappeared so quickly, maybe I wouldn't have had a reason to be looking at someone else," Curtis responded.

Devan blushed. Curtis asked her to dance. For a white girl, Devan really could dance. They danced all night. Once the party was over, Curtis asked Devan if he could walk her to the car, and she replied, "My husband might get angry if he sees me walking out of the club with you."

Curtis backed off. "Oh, I'm sorry. I didn't realize you were married."

"Got you," Devan said, laughing. "You are so gullible."

Curtis looked at her and said, "So I guess I can really walk you to your car?"

"Of course," she answered.

Curtis walked Amber and Devan out to their cars. Amber said good-bye and sped off. Curtis and Devan stood there and talked for another hour or so. Before she got in the car, she kissed Curtis on the cheek and thanked him for a wonderful evening.

30

The Event

The next day began cloudy. Curtis thought that the event might be cancelled due to rain, but the rain never came. Curtis arrived at the beach before any of his coworkers. He had told his assistant to meet him there around seven so that they could start setting up the area designated for their company. Curtis and Byron started putting the tent together and were waiting on someone to run to the store for ice. His coworkers started to stream in as Curtis finished setting up the tent.

Curtis's assistant still hadn't made it, and he began to worry. He knew that she didn't know the area well, and he hoped that she wasn't lost. When he called her, no one answered. Curtis looked up at the cloudy sky, realizing she had to come from far away. Perhaps she had just decided to stay home due to the weather, he thought. Curtis had a lot of work to do anyway, and worrying about a married woman was not at the top of the list.

Devan showed up then with her friend and said she'd be more than happy to make the store run. Devan asked the whereabouts of his faithful assistant, but Curtis didn't respond, thanking her instead for helping out. As the teams arrived, the clouds parted, and the sun came out. It was turning out to be a beautiful day.

Since Curtis's assistant never showed, he recruited Devan, who turned out to be quite efficient. He was on two events but found himself doing a lot of running around to prepare. He had to make sure everyone showed up at the assigned event. He took most of the photographs, and he had to make sure there were enough refreshments at all times.

It had gotten hot, and it was important that everyone stayed hydrated. Curtis had signed him and Devan up for the kayak race and the tube dash. The tube dash consisted of six people, two women and four guys. Curtis didn't have a chance to bond with Devan on this event since it was a team event. The kayaking went a little differently. It was a two-person event requiring equal effort from each partner. Curtis hadn't kayaked in ages, and he had forgotten how intense the workout was. Devan was actually in better shape than Curtis, and it was evident halfway through the event when he accidentally flipped the kayak and had to proceed in flipping back over, which took up his remaining strength. Curtis hopped in the kayak and lay down to try to catch his breath. Not to finish completely last, Devan leaped out of the kayak, grabbed the rope, and pulled it to shore while he was still laid up, gasping for air. The race hadn't ended the way Curtis had anticipated. He had hoped for victory.

It pleased him though the way she took control when he had fallen short. It made him want to know her. They stayed close to each other, spending the rest of the day together. When it was over, Devan accompanied Curtis back to his suite. He didn't want to drive home after a long day at the beach, and he was also hoping to get lucky. He and Devan talked for a while before she left, and he was alone in the room.

Curtis was actually more tired than he thought. The next thing he remembered was the housekeeper waking him up the next morning with a check out warning. Curtis woke up and called Devan to say good morning and thank her for a pleasant day. Curtis called her cell, but there was no answer. He didn't have her home number. Curtis guessed she was seeing somebody else and tried to forget it.

The next day at work Curtis received an e-mail from Devan, asking him to take a break with her. Curtis was hesitant. He had never openly dated a white woman before. He didn't know how they would handle the work situation. Curtis didn't respond right away, and she sent another e-mail. "Are you there today?" the e-mail read.

Curtis knew that he would have to answer her. He finally realized that he was being silly. They had not even decided that they would be in a relationship, and he was already tripping. He e-mailed that he would meet her. They met in the main break room, and everybody seemed to be there. He grew uncomfortable and wondered if people would think they were seeing each other. He knew everyone who'd attended the event and the party had seen them side by side nearly the entire time. He worried that people were already talking about it. This now would just confirm their rumors. When Curtis sat down with Devan, he could feel the stares. Devan, meanwhile, acted oblivious. She evidently had dated outside of her race and was used to people's reactions. Curtis knew that he would be taking a big step when he sat down beside her. He had already had enough drama at work; this was the last thing he needed.

After a few minutes talking to her, Curtis started to feel a little better. She had the prettiest eyes in the building. The few times he and Devan talked, they had had interesting conversations. They shared so much in common. Curtis couldn't believe they would have so much in common growing up as differently as they had.

Before Curtis got up to go back to his office, he grabbed Devan's hand and kissed it. He wanted to let her know how much he liked her. He knew he would turn a few heads with this gesture, but he didn't give a shit. From that day on, Devan and Curtis took their breaks together, either sitting in the café or walking around the building. He got a little slack from some of the black women in the complex, but that was their low self-esteem. Anyway, Devan made him happy.

31

Caribbean Fest

C urtis had to get up a little earlier than usual for a Saturday morning, but he awoke with great expectations. The hurricane season was in full swing. The last two days had poured on them over 6 inches of rain. He rolled out of bed and eyed the sky for some signal of change. He had made plans to help Leonardo install his vertical blinds. Once finished he would go to the store and spend the money made on a pair of shorts to wear to the Caribbean Festival.

The Caribbean Festival was the first big event of the summer. Devan and Curtis had decided to go together. It was an outdoor event, however, so the weather had to cooperate. Curtis looked up at the sky again. It was bright. The signs were good. Curtis had lived in this area for most of his life. He could tell what type of day lay in store by the arrangement of the clouds. It looked to him like the rain had cleared. He was looking forward to spending some quality time with Devan. They had never technically gone out, so he would finally get to see what he was dealing with outside of work.

Curtis had a lot to do that morning, so he brushed his teeth, threw on some old work clothes, and headed over to Leonardo's house. He remembered telling Leonardo that he would be over early. Curtis hoped he wouldn't find his friend still in bed. After pulling onto the drive, Curtis honked his horn to alert him that he was out there and then went to the door. Curtis hated coming to anybody's place so early in the morning, even if he was expected.

Leonardo's wife opened the door and invited him in. She told Curtis that Leonardo was in the bathroom. Curtis made his way back to the room where they were going to be installing the verticals and started reading the directions. Curtis had installed these same blinds several times, but always had to read the directions to make sure he was doing it right. He skimmed over the directions for a few minutes before Leonardo came in, and they started to hang the blinds. Curtis told him that they would have to hurry and finish because he had plans in a couple of hours.

It was a piece of cake with two people. Curtis happily thought that he would be on his way in no time. They finished at noon. Curtis went home to clean up his house, take a shower, and get ready to go to the park. Then, he went to Stein Mart and bought a pair of shorts with the money Leonardo had paid him for helping.

Devan called and asked what time they were going to meet. Curtis told her if she came to his place at three o'clock, they could get there around four. She was early and arrived around two forty-five. Curtis was excited about seeing her outside of her work clothes and in attire that would show some skin. The day at the beach, she had worn a wrap around her bathing suit and hadn't taken it off at anytime to impress anyone. They all knew that they would be running around all day, and to get dressed up would have been a waste of time.

They had agreed to meet at his house because it was only a few miles away from the park. She arrived looking stunning. Her tan and hair were perfect, and her nails and toes were freshly manicured. She wore the blue outfit that enhanced her beautiful blue eyes. When she noticed that Curtis's jaw dropped looking at her, she flashed those pearly whites on him that took him over the top. He could not get over how attracted he was to this woman who wasn't of African descent. There were indeed black women paler than her in skin, so it wasn't that she wasn't a woman of color after all.

Curtis gave her a hug and welcomed her into his house. She immediately made herself at home. He already liked that. Curtis had nothing to hide. Devan looked around as if it all was familiar to her. Curtis could tell the difference now. Black women were always on their guard once they'd entered. Some had been afraid to take their shoes off, and others asked you before they'd do anything no matter what it was. Even after coming over a few times, they would still ask to go to the bathroom or get something out of the fridge. Maybe they thought that they might come across something that was none of their business. Curtis never understood those kinds of manners. Devan, on the other hand, made herself completely at home. He felt her trust immediately, something he had never felt with a black woman. He looked at her sitting on his couch with her feet up and realized no matter how long this affair lasted, he would get more out of it than any other relationship in his life.

Curtis watched with a grin as she fixed herself a glass of Kool-Aid. "She's even drinking my Kool-Aid," he thought. He felt now he did not know anything about white girls because here was a white girl standing in his kitchen drinking his Kool-Aid, and he'd thought that white girls didn't even know what Kool-Aid was. Before she had finished the glass, Curtis was up and had slipped an arm around her. He had called a taxi. He'd decided he'd hold onto her like this until the taxi arrived. This was the first person that he felt completely comfortable with so soon. He didn't have to worry about her going home to her man, and he, himself, didn't have to run off home to anybody. He had forgotten how it felt to be with someone without restrictions.

When they arrived at the Caribbean Fest, they arrived as a couple, hand in hand. Curtis looked into a sea of black faces, aware of the obstacle that might lie ahead. Some of his friends would be caught off guard, he supposed. Devan was looking so good though, it didn't take him long to forget about his surroundings and become completely absorbed with her. The day was perfect. Devan and Curtis had a wonderful time. She loved being out in the sun, she loved the Caribbean music, and she loved being with him.

Curtis even got a slight tan although that was the last thing he needed. The music at the fest was excellent as usual. The Caribbean girls really knew how to move their hips. Curtis could dance himself, but he couldn't match the moves those islanders had in them. Devan actually started laughing at him when she checked him out trying to keep up.

"That's the best you can do?" she asked.

"Let's see if you can do it, Miss White Girl."

Curtis assumed Devan wouldn't have much rhythm. She turned to face him and grabbed his hands. She started moving her hips in a circular motion and put Curtis to shame. It was evident that she had been there before and more than once. Devan was dancing just as well as those girls from the island, *Mon*. She seemed to be a natural. The more she shook those hips, the more Curtis tried to imagine what it would be like to sleep with her. As everyone turned to watch Devan move her ass, Curtis kept on watching but now with a sense of pride.

When the event was over, Curtis tried to hail a taxi, not realizing how difficult the task could be. Devan stood back, apparently finding comedy in his failure. After about fifteen minutes, Curtis gave up. He went over to Devan and told her that he would try again in a couple of minutes and that he didn't want to leave her alone for too long. They took a stroll down by the water and bought ice cream to pass the time. As they walked, Curtis grabbed her hand and thought back to a time before when he would have never considered dating a white woman.

Now here he was, walking hand and hand with one eating ice cream and having a good time at it. He remembered looking at mixed relationships from the outside. He had always wondered why a black guy would date a white woman. Well, his questions were now answered. Was Curtis getting deeper? Here he was, realizing that he wasn't looking to date a white woman, he was looking to date a woman and Devan was surely that and in more ways than one. Curtis grabbed her hand a little tighter, looked her in the eyes, and motioned her to take a lick from his cone. She quickly responded as she put her cone up to his lips. They looked like a couple in a damned ice cream commercial or something. Curtis pulled on her hand, wrapped his other hand around her waist, pulled her close, and gave her the most passionate kiss so far.

"Wow, Devan said. "Where did that come from?"

"I just wanted you to know that I am glad to be here with you, and I believe that you are the most beautiful lady here today." Devan blushed causing her tan to turn this funny shade of red, almost pomegranate. In both a seductive and sarcastic tone, she said then, "Now, let me get us a taxi."

Curtis folded his arms and stood back as she worked her magic. The moment she waved her hands, two taxis stopped at the same time. "Well, are you coming, or are you just going to stand there?"

Curtis ran over to the taxi, and they continued their kiss in the car. By the time they got back to Curtis's house, it was time for Devan to pick up her daughter. She decided not to even go inside because she didn't want the evening to go any further than it had already gone, and she couldn't be late. Curtis respected her decision and told her he would see her at work on Monday.

32

The Truth about Anne's Scare

On Curtis's annual visit to his doctor, he got a call a couple of days later and was asked to come into the office. He had gone to the doctor's office for over thirty years and was never called to come in to go over his test results. When he got the call, the nurse asked when a good time for him to come in was. He asked for the next available appointment. He knew that he could not go more than two days without knowing what in the hell was going on. She made an appointment for the next morning. The only thoughts running through his mind revolved around unprotected sex.

He didn't sleep at all the night before the appointment. At five in the morning, he was taking a shower as if whatever he had could be washed away. Curtis got to the office before the doctor and his nurse. He tried to get information out of the nurse, but she informed him that he would have to wait for the doctor. The wait seemed to last an eternity. He was glad that he hadn't slept with Devan at this point. Curtis would normally use condoms, but there were a few times he didn't. He knew better.

Every time he remembered that he hadn't used a condom, he hit himself in the head. Curtis knew the nurse thought he was losing his mind, but he guessed she had seen this type of behavior before. She whispered that everything would be okay, and he got the impression from her that everything would really be okay. Based on the comment from the nurse, he knew that whatever it was, it wasn't fatal a least. That eased his mind a little. What else could it be then if it wasn't fatal?

Curtis didn't have any symptoms. He felt fine. After the doctor called him, he asked, "Do you practice safe sex?"

He asked him how many partners had he had in the past year. That was easy. The only person Curtis had been with without a condom was Anne. They had never used a condom. Hell, he figured that she was safe because she was married, and he had been married so long that it would be okay. What he didn't seem to realize was that if she could be with him and not use a condom, he couldn't be sure that she had done the same with someone else. Logic never seems to enter into the equation when hormones are raging. Curtis made himself a promise that if he got out of this bullshit, he would always use a condom, forever and always! The doctor told Curtis that he had contracted a STD that was common and treatable without side effects. He also told him to inform his sex partners about the STD. He said that women could carry the disease with few or no symptoms. Curtis gave him his word that he would tell anyone he had sex with to make sure they got treated.

When Curtis got home, he remembered what Anne had said about her visit to the doctor. Suddenly it all made sense. He went on the Internet and e-mailed her an article about the STD. She replied thanks, and he never heard from her again. Curtis imagined that this must have continued the drama she had been going on with Ty, but he had to tell her what he knew. After Curtis brief research of the STD he sent Anne a email that read:

Trichomoniasis, a sexually transmitted disease affects 170 million people worldwide each year. . They identified 26,000 confirmed genes in Trichomonas vaginalis and say there may be an additional 34,000 unconfirmed genes. In women, the parasite attaches to the vaginal lining and sends tendril-like projections into the tissue. Trichomonas vaginalis also secretes proteins that destroy the cells that make up the tissue of the vaginal lining. Genital itching, vaginal discharge, inflamed cervix

*and pain during urination or intercourse are among the symptoms expe-
rienced by women infected with the parasite, according to background
information in a news release. Acute infection is associated with pelvic
inflammatory disease, and trichomoniasis increases a woman's risk of
being infected with HIV, the virus that causes AIDS. Pregnant women
with trichomoniasis are more likely to have premature babies or babies
with low birth weight. Men infected with the parasite may experience
mild symptoms such as a burning sensation after urination and may suffer urogenital infections such as urethritis and prostatitis.*

33

Nobody Is Alone

urtis and Devan were more than ever fueled for their fiery exchanges, for learning more and more about each other. Curtis grew increasingly curious about the secrets she might have. Experience had shown him that there was always the possibility of a ripple, no matter how small the pebble thrown or the insignificance of the secret kept. Devan's ten-year-old daughter told her mother she liked Curtis. Curtis had turned Devan's birthday into a family affair by showing up at Jayde's school beforehand with a present for Jayde to wrap and give to her mother.

Although Devan had dated several guys in the ten years since becoming a single parent, she had been cautious about whom she exposed to Jayde. As sincere as the relationship with Curtis seemed to be, Devan in the first few months hesitated about any moves that involved Jayde and whatever emotional commitments or catastrophes were likely in having her daughter know her boyfriend. Curtis, conscious that Devan as a routine asked him over only after Jayde had already gone to bed, asked, "Is it true that you don't want me to know your daughter?"

Devan looked at Curtis with her blue eyes and with all sincerity explained that Jayde was all she had. She couldn't risk just letting anyone into her life and upsetting the life they had built. "Do you think I'm capable of that, Devan?" Curtis asked.

"I'm not sure, Curtis, but this is new to us, and until I get to know you better, I have to have it this way."

Curtis was thoughtful for a minute. He said, "I understand, Devan, and I respect your decision, but keep in mind that we are good for each other, and I believe that I can be good for Jayde as well. I want to be able to spend more time with you and your daughter. My coming to your house at odd times of the morning makes me feel as though I'm sneaking around messing with someone's wife. And when I do get here, you always act as if you are expecting someone."

Devan looked at Curtis and said, "I'm sorry that it has to be this way, but Jayde gets really attached to people, and I can tell she already likes you. I think its best that you see her as little as possible right now." Curtis could tell she was trying to be gentle. Nevertheless, the message was bitter.

"Okay," Curtis muttered, "I have to respect that."

"Curtis, can I tell you something without you judging or thinking badly of me?"

Curtis realized a confession was at his feet. "What is it, Devan? And, no, I won't judge you."

"You mentioned earlier that you always felt as though I was expecting someone when you are here at night. I'm not sure where you got that from, but you are somewhat right."

She had his undivided attention. Devan continued, "Well, the fact of the matter is, I had been seeing this person for over a year, and he would come over at night. However, I ended that relationship when we started seeing each other and haven't heard from him since."

Curtis interrupted, "So why do you always stare at the door as if he might come and knock on it at anytime?"

"I didn't realize that I was doing that, but I will try and be a little more comfortable from now on," Devan said.

"So if you had been seeing him for so long, why did you end it now—because I came along? We haven't really established things," Curtis said.

"Well, regardless of what we have established, Curtis, it will still be more than what he and I can have."

Curtis was puzzled for a few seconds. Then, he had his epiphany. "He's married, huh?"

"Yes, he is, and I have been trying to break it off for quite some time now, but it gets difficult."

"Well, why did you get involved with him in the first place?" Curtis knew the answer. He quickly followed up. "Does he work with us?"

"He told me he wasn't married when we met, and I had no reason not to believe him. No, he doesn't work with us."

"He spent a lot of time here. We went out a couple nights a week doing all those things couples do. Jayde got to know him, and I let my defenses down. Then all of a sudden, while he is here, a woman calls asking for him."

Curtis's eyebrow arched from the intrigue of Devan's story. "After a few seconds on the phone, he looked at me and confessed that he was married, that she had found my number on his phone bill. Oh, he apologized and all that. He promised that she would never call my number again. The express point of her calling was so that he would explain himself and come clean with me."

Curtis knew how trifling men could be—he had been one all his life. "So why didn't you stop the relationship when you found out about it?" Curtis asked.

Devan looked at him with a blank expression on her face and said, "I don't know."

Although Curtis kept quiet, he felt he knew and possibly she too knew why, even if she couldn't say why just yet. Curtis had learned since his divorce that there seemed to be many more available women than men on that side of the chain link fence. Possibly Devan had been willing to accept what she could get when she could get it. Curtis finally said, "Well, I'm not married, and there will be no surprise phone calls, okay?"

"So you don't think any differently of me because of my involvement with a married man?"

Curtis looked at Devan and said with sincerity, "Listen, I can't start to judge you. We're all human. I know I've made countless mistakes. People are going to do whatever it takes to get them to the next day.

Sometimes, we do crazy shit. All I know of you is how you're handling our relationship. If there is something I can't deal with, I will tell you, and we will try and work it out. We can only start from here, where we are now." Curtis reached over, pulled Devan into his chest, and said, "We are going to be all right, and I hope you have a wonderful birthday tomorrow, just in case I don't see you."

"It's a little too late to try and stay away now. I already know about the gift you got for Jayde. I can't tell you how much that meant to her, and to me. She told me straight out that I had to invite you to my celebration."

Curtis was astonished. "She told you about the gift. I told her not to say anything," Curtis said.

"Well, you must remember when your kids were ten. Come on, think about it," Devan said.

"Okay, I guess you're right. I guess I should have known that there'd be a good chance that she would tell you."

Devan looked into Curtis's eyes and said, "Please don't hurt us. God knows we have been through a lot, and I don't want to see the look on my daughter's face if I have to tell her that you won't be coming around anymore."

Curtis said, "That's not my intention, Devan. Hell, I could say the same thing to you."

Devan just melted into his arms, and they made love.

34
Devan's Special

Once Curtis and Devan had made love, their relationship started to blossom. Curtis learned to dismiss the inevitable stares. He began to take no notice of what the black women on the streets would whisper walking past. He had found a wonderful person, and color didn't have anything to do with anything. One by one, the stereotypes crumbled. Curtis learned that Devan was neither passive nor submissive. She was as strong as any black woman, and for possibly the first time in his adult life, he was genuinely happy around her.

She loved just to satisfy him. Devan was as unreserved when it came to loving as any woman could be. They went through some experiences that Curtis, even after Janice and Anne, had classified as movie material. They essentially lost their minds for the first six weeks of the relationship. They couldn't keep their hands off each other. Devan would send Curtis e-mails to let him know that she wasn't wearing any underwear, that she wanted him to meet her in the elevator. Once there, they hit the emergency button and made love right in the elevator up to the time of rescue. As for lunch, lunch was always an experience. It didn't matter where they went, they would end up in someone's restroom locking hips.

Curtis and Devan both lived close to work, but they more often preferred the daring of public places to the sanctity of home for their rendezvous. They sought excitement, and excitement lay in the hills, in any place where there was danger in being seen or caught. They were living on the edge and didn't care about anyone outside of their circle. On a rare day that Devan and Curtis went to her house for lunch for her leftovers, Devan was in the process of placing the food in the microwave as Curtis attacked her from behind.

"Curtis," she said, "not today, baby. It's a bad time for mama."

Curtis said, "Damn, that's okay. I don't need any, but can I get a kiss?"

Consenting, Devan turned around and gave him the most passionate kiss she could. Feeling his nature rise through his pants, she pushed him away.

"Come on. Let's eat, Curtis, so we can get back to work." They sat down, ate lunch, and began heading back to work. Devan noticed though that Curtis was still rock hard when they got into the car. "How are you going to go back to work like that?" she asked.

"Oh, I will be okay," Curtis said. "I will just have to take my shirt out of my pants for a while."

Devan looked at Curtis with a devilish smile and said, "I will take care of it for you." As Curtis drove, Devan reached over and unzipped his pants, pulled out his rod, and started to rub up and down his shaft. This was turning him on even more. By the time they pulled into the complex's parking garage, Curtis was in worse shape than before. Curtis parked and sat back, and Devan bent over and took his penis into her mouth. Curtis stopped her. "Hey, what are you doing girl? We are out in the open here. Someone might see us."

Devan looked at Curtis, the devil still in her, and said, "You just keep your eyes open and let me handle this."

Before he knew it, Devan was going up and down on his dick right there in the parking lot. For the first minute or two, Curtis was extremely nervous. It didn't take long, however, for Devan's expert lips to perform for desired effect. Curtis soon forgot about work, the garage, the daylight, submerged completely and at once in their sex escapade. It took only another minute for Curtis to reach an orgasm. As he started to come, he tried to push Devan away, not wanting to come in her mouth. Curtis had never been involved with a black woman willing to take one for the team, so he had grown accustomed to pushing them away. Devan, meanwhile, would not take it out of her mouth. "Devan, I'm about to come," Curtis said.

The moment he mentioned those words, Devan sped up her movements. She was milking Curtis and had no intention of pulling back. He realized the plan then and showed her he was all for it with an eager nod. Then, he put his head back and held on for the ride. Curtis's toes almost shot through his Stacys when he peaked. He couldn't believe how intense it was. "Damn, girl, what are you trying to do to me? Drive me crazy or something?" Curtis asked her.

Devan just looked up at Curtis and said, "Ah, that was good." She got out of the car and left him there to regroup. As he sat there trying to get his clothes together, Janice passed by and winked. Curtis was sure she had seen it all. This was the last person Curtis needed to see this. She was just enough of a bitch to go to HR and report him. Curtis now had to think quickly. He knew that by the time he got back to his desk, Janice would have already contacted HR. Then, it'd be his word against hers, and everybody would know she had reason to lie. Curtis went through the different scenarios and decided he could provide an answer for whatever could be laid against him.

To Curtis's surprise, Janice never did go to HR. Instead, she alerted them to the prospect of misconduct. She told HR that she had seen two people in the parking lot having sex without naming anyone or providing a description of the vehicle. Curtis received a universal e-mail from HR stating that any unauthorized behavior on company grounds was terms for immediate termination. Janice printed the e-mail out and wrote across the top of it: "Don't think I don't have pictures!" And left it on Curtis's windshield.

Curtis couldn't believe that he let this shit happen to him. He never responded to Janice and never heard from her either. Then again, he did everything in his power not to cross her path ever again.

Devan had grown so close to Curtis that Jayde now too was comfortable and familiar with Curtis. Devan then took him to her parents' house. He could tell after the introduction that though they were trying to accept a black man in their daughter's life, they weren't exactly happy about it. They were cordial and polite. Curtis had heard their story from Devan and formed his own assumptions about Germans and what or how much they'd tolerate. It was prejudice no less, and Curtis realized this, but their love for Jayde made Curtis a little more comfortable with the idea of being in their home. Primarily, he hoped they wouldn't say anything to embarrass him or Devan.

Curtis was no racist, but somehow, the knowledge that they were aware of him screwing their daughter made him want to cringe in their presence. Fortunately, the plan for the night was a movie to start. There'd be no conversation to worry about. Someday he'd really have to talk to them, but for now, this was exactly what he would have planned. Curtis really liked Devan, so what her parents thought about him was important to him. It was a strange sight, the two Germans babysitting their granddaughter who was more black than white. Her parents probably never envisioned that someday, their redheaded little girl would bring home a black boyfriend, Curtis thought.

Life is funny this way. More and more of these white grandparents are raising mixed grandchildren, and as time goes on, more and more of us will come from mixed and diverse backgrounds. Curtis had seen a lot of racism in his own life. Despite the changes, he understood how alive it still was, if only alive as embers.

He was just happy to have witnessed in his lifetime the changes that were occurring to close some of the old gaps. If there was still a long way to go, at least society had embarked. Curtis got so used to Devan's parents, he visited them even without her. After a few months, Devan began to hint about the future. She wanted Curtis to make more of a commitment. Devan had never been married and had brought other guys to meet her parents before. She told him she believed that they liked Curtis more than any of the others. "You know, Curtis, I have kissed enough frogs in my life to know that you are truly my knight," Devan said.

They were on their daily stroll around the work complex. Curtis sighed. He knew he was unable to commit just yet. He noticed that Devan had started to make these comments regularly though. Curtis so far had blown off a lot of the pressure, but this time, she seemed particularly serious. She was letting him know he was what she wanted. "But why me?" Curtis asked.

"I just think you are a kind and sincere person. Genuine, you know? They're qualities you just don't find anymore," Devan explained.

Her words comforted him, but at the same time, the more she pushed, the more he pulled back. He could feel himself pulling away from her. He liked Devan, but he didn't want to start talking marriage, and he could tell that's where she was going.

Curtis realized that he had to find a weakness in her, something that he could use as an excuse to slow down their relationship, , and to do it without Devan figuring it out. One night Curtis got his wish. Devan and he had gone out to one of her girlfriends' house to watch a big fight. There was a lot of food and drink. He could remember the way Devan drank. She knew that Curtis was driving, and she was in the company of her friends. Out of comfort, she drank and drank. The more she drank, the more she adapted the tin man concept. The more oil she had, the looser she became. Unlike the black women Curtis had known, Devan became friendlier and touchier the more she drank. It didn't seem to matter who was around. Curtis in his sober mind watched as Devan flirted with another man. Whether it was innocent or not, Curtis couldn't help getting upset about it. At one point, she actually followed the guy into the bathroom, and that totally blew Curtis's mind. He said nothing that night. But the next day, he confronted her. Devan had no clue that she had done the things he had noticed and was asking her about. She became apologetic. Curtis explained to her that she had embarrassed him. He told her he didn't think that she had handled herself as if she were in love with anyone.

Devan listened for a while and then asked if this meant Curtis was breaking up with her. Without having premeditated the decision, Curtis knew she was right. He was breaking up. At the same time, he didn't want to end it just like that.

"Devan, I really like you, and I don't want us to break up, but I think we are just moving too fast. We should just take this thing day by day and see what happens," Curtis said.

Devan had been around long enough to realize that when someone says, "let's take it day by day," it was a nice way of saying, "this isn't working very well." Devan gave Curtis the blank look he knew so well and said, "Okay."

In the weeks that followed, Curtis and Devan slowed their pace. They didn't see much of each other anymore. Even when Curtis went by her house, he could feel a difference in the way Jayde spoke to him. It was evident that Devan had said something to her to embitter her against him. Maybe she had started preparing her for the breakup. He had really started feeling bad. He had become attached to Devan and her daughter. He had stepped in and taken on the role of the father and didn't want to hurt Jayde or her mother. He decided against his better judgment to stick around and try to make it work. Devan wasn't a bad girl, he rationalized. She just wanted to get married, and he wasn't ready. What was so bad about that? In hindsight, Curtis might have been better off heading for the hills, but he didn't. Instead, he stayed until he had their hearts. He stayed until it was assumed that this was for good. Then, when he couldn't take any more staying, he told Devan that she deserved someone who'd make her a bride.

Without bells, alarms, whistles, or warnings, Curtis just stopped calling and visiting. There were days when Devan called Curtis over and over again, and he'd never answered. Finally, she left a message to tell him that he should have at least been man enough to break up with her in person instead of taking the coward's way out. She told him she had never been treated that way before and that it was the last thing she'd expected of him.

Curtis knew that everything she was saying was true. He also knew that if he had talked to Devan in person, she would have used his kindness as a crutch. He wouldn't have had the discipline to go through with it. The message tore his heart out, but didn't change his mind. Breaking up the coward's way had been a necessary evil, and he'd had to do it. Curtis and Devan never talked again. Last he heard she was engaged to Chad, a nice white guy from work. Devan, who hadn't dated a white guy in twenty years, finally found her groom after twenty years spent in the arms of black men. Go figure, Curtis thought.

35
Meeting Demetria

T he first encounter with Demetria came five days before the end of the fiscal year, which meant Curtis met Demetria while everyone was running around in panic mode. This was by far the most crucial time in the business. In order for the yearly numbers to be in line for the stockholders, everyone's job was magnified threefold. Although there were eleven months in the year, most of the work was done in the last two weeks. All the sales people were busting chops to make the extra sales, which would ripple throughout the entire company. Curtis was responsible for the equipment inventory for the Northeast region and had to make sure each piece was in its respective warehouse.

All Monday morning, he had been waiting on a fax from the Newark office regarding an incorrect shipment. The order was part of a $2 million sale that was in jeopardy because the vendor had sent the wrong machine. He needed proof of the mistake so he would have the leverage to force them to send the right machine and by overnight delivery. Curtis had asked the warehouse to fax him a copy of the shipping log so that he could compare it to the purchase order he had sent. After his third trip to the fax machine, he worried that if he did not have the fax by noon, there'd be no way to have the correct shipment in to him for tomorrow. He knew that the crew at the warehouse was also overworked and understaffed, that for them too, this was the busiest time of the year.

Regardless, he needed the fax and he needed it now. Storming his way back to his office, he literally almost knocked down Demetria. If he hadn't caught her, she would have definitely hit the floor. Demetria was a petite young lady with everything Curtis liked in all the right places. When he caught her, they found themselves wrapped up in each other's arms, in a somewhat awkward and suggestive position.

"I'm sorry," Curtis said. "I didn't realize anyone was here."

All year, Curtis had noticed no one in that particular cube situated en route to the fax, and he'd been used to cutting the corner close there to save a little time.

"Yeah, this is my first day," Demetria explained.

As he released her having helped her to her feet, Curtis welcomed her to the company and continued confusedly back to his desk. Now he had forgotten what he was in such a hurry to do. The only thing he could think about was the girl in the hall that he had held in his arms. The warmth of her body seemed to linger upon him. She had about seven or eight corn-rows in her hair all braided front to back. She wore a fitted blue shirt with a pleasant flower print. Her arms were long and thin, exposed by the half sleeves of the blouse that she'd paired with baggy blue jeans. It was the last week of the year, so all the employees were permitted to dress down. Her outfit didn't do anything for her, but because of their close contact, Curtis could tell that she had a lot going on underneath.

Her smile was like a ray of sunshine after a long span of rain. Curtis shook his head a couple of times to clear the visions that occupied his mind. He picked up the phone. It dawned on him finally what he'd been trying to get accomplished. Once Curtis got back into his groove, the memory of their encounter faded. Over the next several days, he didn't see Demetria again. She was relocated to a more permanent desk after a few days in the corner where he'd stumbled upon her. Although she had only moved two cubes down, he had no reason to travel in that direc-tion. It would be a couple of weeks before he saw her again. Their paths would cross again in the most unlikely way.

The company was sponsoring ten seats at the Annual Business Leaders Banquet. These seats were to be given out on a first come first served basis. Curtis had participated every year for the past three years, so he had no problem getting his ticket. Curtis was a friend of the new president, John Dennison, and was proud to see that he had risen over the adversity that had plagued him in his younger days. Although John was an attorney, he had gotten himself involved in drugs during his wife's long fight and ultimate defeat from cancer. It took a while after her death for John to become more focused than ever. He did so and was eventually voted in the president of the Business Leaders Association.

Curtis was running a little late to the event. To get to his chair, he picked and stumbled across aisles and tables. John noticed him and made a quick joke about his tardiness as Curtis found his chair. Before making it into the chair, he lost his balance and found himself fumbling to hang onto the back of a chair that was occupied. When he looked up, he stared into Demetria's eyes.

"We have to stop meeting this way," she said.

Very embarrassed, Curtis said, "You must think I'm the clumsiest person you've ever met."

"No, I just think you are trying to get next to me," she answered.

Curtis stood up and straightened his jacket. "I am sorry," he said. "I have a better game than that anyway," he added.

"This must be your seat," Demetria said, motioning to the seat where she had laid her purse. "I was saving it for you," she said, removing the little clutch.

Curtis thanked her and sat down. They spent the rest of the night talking as if they had known each other for years. They were both surprised by how well they got along. After the banquet, Curtis walked her to her car. He hinted that if ever she were interested, he would like to get to know her better. Curtis didn't want to be stuck classified and labeled as a big brother, so he flirted with her every chance he got. After a few months, he and Demetria were inseparable. They took breaks together, lunched together, and were even caught frequenting each other's desk a few times throughout each day. Demetria had real affection for Curtis. It seemed to him that she must have wondered in the back of her mind nevertheless what it would be like to jump his bones.

One day when Curtis walked her to her car, she gave him a hug before he went back into the office. She hadn't realized that Curtis was as solid as he was.

"Man, you must work out," Demetria said.

"Yeah, I hit the gym a few times a week. You should join me," he said.

"Naw, I get my workout on when I go out. I use dancing as my workout routine," she said.

"If that works for you," Curtis answered. "You look good anyway. You really don't need to go to the gym until you're in your forties and the metabolism slows down. Wait until then."

Demetria knew that she needed to work out more, but she employed every excuse not to go. She still had her figure and her youth, and working out seemed to her something for the distant future.

36

The Day of the Big Storm

A roar of thunder followed the streak of lightning. Curtis and Demetria were sitting in the café on their morning break. Demetria had never been a big fan of the rumble in the skies. Before the thunder subsided, Demetria was up and out of her seat.

"Where are you going?" Curtis asked.

"I am going to sit over here. You know how much I hate thunder and lightning," Demetria answered.

"Girl, if God wanted you today, he would get you. Moving to the center of the room won't help." Curtis laughed.

"Well, I feel a lot better over here anyway. Are you coming?"

Curtis laughed again as he followed Demetria over to the other table. He could recall his mother closing all the windows and curtains whenever it would storm as if that would stop the lightning from hitting their house. She would also forbid anyone to talk on the phone, to move around needlessly, or take a shower. In so many ways, Demetria reminded Curtis of being a boy and the things that his mother had taught him.

"What are you laughing about?" Demetria asked.

"It's just funny how some of the things you do bring back childhood memories that I had completely forgotten about." There were so many other things that Demetria had done to give Curtis the old feeling of being young. He felt he could fall for her, this woman who was brought up the same way he had been.

"Well, I am afraid of lightning, and I am not going to stay by that window with it acting up outside like that," Demetria continued. She was a few years younger than Curtis. It did not occur to her that they had their histories in common.

The storm was uncommonly violent for winter. The strongest lightning storms typically did not occur until springtime. A huge streak of lightning followed by the loudest crack of thunder yet whipped upon them. Demetria jumped as the lights in the café blinked. They were out for a second or two, and Demetria found herself clutching Curtis's hand. She let out a small scream.

"It's okay," Curtis said. "There is no way that lightning can hit you inside this building. Not unless it's your time to go, and if that's the case, it will find you no matter what."

Demetria let his hand go and looked at him as if she didn't like him taking the storm so lightly. Storms had never frightened Curtis. He thought of them simply as nature's way of throwing a temper tantrum. Actually, he wished the storms would come more often when he and Demetria were together. It wasn't often he got a chance to hold her hand. Curtis gathered up the trash from their breakfasts.

"Ready to go?" he asked Demetria.

"Do we have to go back right now?" she moaned. She was still trying to wait out the storm.

"You know that this storm is here to stay, right?" Curtis asked. He knew some storms went on for hours. Curtis grabbed her hand and helped her to her feet. Just as she rose up from the chair, the thunder clapped in a series of repeating explosions. Instinctively, she reached out, threw her arms around Curtis, hung on, letting out a slight gasp. The lights went out for about ten seconds. When they suddenly came back on, Demetria realized how closely she was holding Curtis. "Oh, I'm sorry, Curtis. I didn't mean to…"

"Don't worry," Curtis interrupted. "It was my pleasure."

She looked at him as if to say, "You enjoyed that, didn't you? I know what you are thinking about, and yeah, you're right. That was the best hug I have received all year." But instead of saying anything, she walked away. Curtis followed her.

"I will see you around lunchtime, buster," she said.

He gave her the routine peace sign and disappeared around the corner. Curtis never took the elevator when he returned to his desk. There were more scenic routes. Although he had it bad for Demetria, he was as free as a bird, and he made sure the ladies of the office were well aware of that fact. When Curtis entered the staircase, the storm had started to affect the massive concrete structure that contained within its walls about four hundred employees. All the lights were out, and the hallways were dark. Curtis froze for a minute anticipating the lights to come back on. After a few minutes, he decided to try to navigate the staircase in the dark. The emergency lights came on, and he made his way out.

Back at his desk, he found that Demetria had called twice without leaving a message. The office was noisy and brimming with the hectic excitement of people's varied responses to lack of electricity, a raging storm, and sitting around in the dark together. The computers were down. He heard a few curses about lost work. After thirty minutes sitting in the dark at his desk, Curtis decided to return Demetria's call.

"Are you just getting back to your desk?" Demetria asked.

"Yeah, I took the scenic route. Hell, it doesn't matter at this rate. None of the computers are working now," Curtis said, staring into his blank screen. "The last time this happened we were sitting around for hours before we got power again. Let's meet in the cafeteria," Curtis said.

They sat in the cafeteria together for almost an hour in blanket darkness. They had noticed several people leaving by the staircase as if they were going home for the day. Cynthia came over to them and asked if they planned on sitting there all day.

"What are you talking about, Cynthia?" Demetria asked her.

"Everyone has been dismissed to go," Cynthia answered. "If you guys had been in your departments, you would have known." Cynthia stalked off with her purse and car keys dangling in hand.

"See you lovers later," she said from the open stairwell door.

"I'm going to my desk to see what's going on," Curtis said. "I don't want to stay here any longer than I have to."

Curtis got up from his chair and told Demetria that he would call her when he found out what their department was doing. Both of their areas had already been dismissed by the time they returned. Curtis reached for the phone, which started to ring. Demetria, it seemed, had beat him to it.

"So what's up?" Curtis asked.

"Oh, I guess I will just go home and watch TV. At least I will have a peace of mind since my family won't be there."

The rain was coming down even harder than before. Demetria stepped back. "I really don't feel like driving in this rain. The bridge gets scary in all this rain," she said.

Curtis asked her over to his house. "We can order a movie if you want," he said.

Demetria was hesitant, but driving over the bridge was the last thing she wanted to do. After getting a few "I don't knows," Curtis finally said, "Well, when you make up your mind, let me know. I'm going home."

At last, Demetria said, "I'll be behind you."

Curtis smiled. He enjoyed it when she came over. He had never gotten past first base with her, but the challenge was worthwhile. As usual, the moment Demetria walked in the door, she kicked off her shoes, went straight to the bedroom for a comforter and pillow, ran back, and jumped on the couch. "Okay, what are we renting?" she asked.

Curtis sat down on the barstool and watched her until she was comfortable on the sofa. "I don't know yet," he said as he flipped through the channels on the remote. After surfing the pay-per-view stations, they landed on the *40-Year-Old Virgin*. Neither of them had seen it before. They didn't realize either how much sex would be discussed. As they usually did, Curtis sat on one end of the couch, and Demetria curled up on the other. To keep things consistent, he grabbed her feet and started to rub them.

"Why do you always do that when I tell you I don't want you to?" asked Demetria.

"Because you want me to do this. You just don't want me to know that you want me to do this."

She laughed. "You are so silly!"

Curtis had begun to see something in Demetria he had never seen before. The look in her eyes spoke words that he had never heard before.

Assuming his feelings were on point, he asked her to join him over on his end of the couch. She surprised him by coming without hesitating. Curtis was shocked. He'd grown used to making the attempts, but Demetria had never responded to any of his sexually loaded suggestions. He wondered if this would finally be the day. "Wow," Curtis said as he put his arms around her and exhaled deeply. He couldn't recall ever feeling this good in his entire life. He had never touched her in an inappropriate manner, but the more he thought about her, the more he could imagine touching her. Always just a matter of time, Curtis thought.

The movie was filled with sexual innuendoes, and Demetria being nestled up between his legs didn't help at all. After a few minutes, Curtis couldn't handle it anymore. Nature was calling and collecting its toll. He knew that Demetria had noticed that he had begun to get excited, but he didn't say anything, and she didn't either. By now Curtis was hard as a box of jawbreakers, and he couldn't help but to take it to the next level. He knew that she knew he was hard even though she didn't attempt to move away from it at all. He figured he'd try crossing that bridge now. Curtis ran his hand across her chest and got the reaction he'd expected.

"What are you doing?" Demetria asked him.

"Did you expect me not to touch you? I am human, you know."

She didn't protest anymore. She didn't say anything. He interpreted the silence as the light to proceed. He continued to touch her, and she continued to let him. He couldn't believe that she didn't grab her purse and make a beeline to the door as she had done on the many other occasions when he'd gotten a little too frisky.

He reached over and kissed her on the nape of her neck. Again, where he expected protest, he received silence. It was obvious now that she was ready to take their friendship to another level. After a few more neck kisses, she turned over, lay on top of Curtis, looked at him, and said, "I thought we came here to watch a movie."

He reached around her and took her ass in his hands. It was such a nice ass. "Why are you touching my ass, Curtis?" she asked.

"How could I not touch it? You know I have waited over a year to be with you in this way. I'm going to do all you let me do." She just laughed and put her arms around him as he continued to massage her ass. He ran his hand through her hair while stroking her buttocks with his other hand. He started kissing her neck again, but this time he got a reaction out of her.

He thought, "Finally, after all this time, she is finally going to give me a shot at this ass." Curtis put his hands under her shirt and unclasped her bra.

"What are you doing, Curtis?"

"I'm taking loose your bra. Why are you asking that?"

"Because you need to stop," Demetria said.

Curtis got frustrated then. He pushed her away and tried to focus on the movie again. Several minutes passed. "Why are you tripping?" Curtis asked. "You know if you tell me to stop, I will stop."

She just looked at him and said, "You are such a gentleman after all."

He was tired of her calling him a gentleman, however. He grabbed her, threw her on her back, and pressed his body against hers. He put his hand up her shirt and grabbed a handful of breast. She tried to grab his hands, but before she could, he pressed his body again even tighter giving her no room to move. The only thing she could do was put her hands around his waist. "I am tired of you calling me that," he said as he kissed her on her chest above the shirt line, trying to work his way down to her breasts. Here, she stopped his progression. He decided to go for the weak spot he had access to, her earlobes. Once he ran his tongue along the edge of her ear and then placed it in her ear, she grabbed his ass and started to move her hips.

Everything in her wanted to have sex with Curtis, but it was for all the wrong reasons. This screw would be for the satisfaction of an orgasm only. Even though she felt this was what she wanted, she cared far too much for Curtis to give him a taste of something he may never be able to sample again. Then again, perhaps she was afraid that she might like it too much. Although she was having an internal battle with herself, she continued to let Curtis have his way with her. She started to kiss Curtis on his chest. She had always felt that Curtis had a nice chest. To kiss it brought her satisfaction.

All of a sudden though, she told Curtis to get up, that she couldn't let him penetrate her. She rushed to explain how she hadn't meant to let things get this far. Both of them found they were sitting there half naked, wondering what had just happened.

"How could you just stop like that? Do you know what you are doing to me?" Curtis said, now completely frustrated.

"Yeah, I'm sorry. I know I shouldn't have gotten you all worked up. I have to leave anyway."

As Demetria started putting on her clothes, Curtis knew that he would never have another chance. The only thing he could do was watch her, and all chances of him sleeping with her seemed to disappear with every piece of clothing she put on. "So what is the real problem, Demetria?" Curtis asked.

Demetria looked at Curtis, wanting to give him an explanation. She had let him get closer and closer. She had been flattered by his attention and interest. She supposed it was high time he knew her secret. "Curtis, there is something I need to tell you, and I hope that you don't hate me after I tell you."

Curtis was puzzled. He wondered what in the world she could be talking about. They had talked about everything in the past year or so. What could she tell him now that he didn't already know? Demetria looked at him and said, "I'm married."

Curtis was floored. He sank to a puddle. "How could this be?" he said out loud to himself more than to her. "How come you never told me?" Curtis demanded.

Demetria looked at Curtis, embarrassed, and said, "Not sure why I didn't tell you. When we first met, I didn't think we would become this close. Once we started getting closer, I didn't want to lose your friendship. My marriage isn't going well right now, and I thought I wanted this, but I just can't."

Curtis, still in disbelief, could only sit there and shake his head. "Well, I'm glad you told me because if you had gone through with it, you would have taken the decision away from me, and you don't know how I would have felt about that."

By the time her shoes were on, Curtis was feeling the kind of pain he hadn't felt since high school. He actually had a classic case of the blue balls. He still couldn't believe it.

"Well, we can talk about it later, but I must leave now," Demetria said. "Are you going to walk me to the door?"

Curtis was in too much pain to get up. "To be honest with you, I would love to, but I don't think I can," Curtis said.

"I am sorry I put you through that. I will call you later," she said, closing the door behind her.

"Whatever," Curtis said.

Curtis was dumbfounded about how he'd interact with Demetria after that. The bomb she had dropped on him was a big one, and he knew there'd be few ways to make it less awkward. Curtis walked into his office and turned on the little transistor radio next to his monitor to the talk show that always cheered him up. He'd decided that he wasn't going to call Demetria, and he hoped that she wouldn't call him. The way things had gone they were better off leaving things put. But like clockwork, Demetria e-mailed Curtis five minutes before break time and asked whether they'd meet for break. Curtis sat there and stared at his monitor, thinking of how to answer. He began to type when Demetria walked into his office.

"Are you going to answer or what?" she asked.

Startled, Curtis turned around in his chair and looked up at Demetria. "I was just responding. Can you be patient?" he said.

"Well I figured you might not answer or you would just refuse to come, so I decided to come walk you to break."

"If I didn't want to go, I wouldn't, regardless if you came here or not," Curtis answered.

Demetria looked at Curtis. She wanted to apologize about not telling him sooner. She wanted to say a few things or figure out how to patch up what she had broken, but she wanted him to come on break with her first. The door was open, and Curtis knew by the supreme silence around him, that meant only one thing. Everybody was listening. Although Curtis had an office with a door on it, Demetria had left it open, and the last notes of their conversation still seemed to be echoing up and down the hallways. This was as much excitement as they had heard in a while. He could see the funny faces poking past while Demetria stood waiting for him.

Curtis had a lot on his mind by now. He wanted to get all of it off his chest finally in the open air and away from the din of the break room. "Listen Demetria, for the past year we have become very close. I am aware that we never crossed the line, but your lying to me the entire time makes me question our friendship."

"Curtis, the only reason I didn't mention the fact that I was married was because I am not proud of my marriage, and I haven't been happy in years. When I met you, you brought joy back into my life. You possess all the things that I like in a man, and I needed you to help me keep a portion of me intact."

"But, Demetria, you know that I started caring about you, and although we kept our relationship platonic, I could have handled this a little differently had I known."

"How, Curtis? By not spending as much time with me?" she asked.

"Demetria, you used my friendship as a crutch, and you did so without any regard for my feelings. It was wrong. Wrong, Demetria. You and I both know this." Curtis's words rang in his own head. He knew he was being harsh, but he couldn't help it.

Demetria lowered her head and said, "I am truly sorry for not telling you, but I need you in my life right now. Please don't take it out on me. I married this guy for all the wrong reasons, and I am miserable. You are the only light in my life. Don't take that away from me."

Curtis looked in her eyes, and he knew then that he had fallen in love with her. "Listen, Demetria, I will always be there for you. We have been friends for over a year. I guess I never expected anything like this. I just don't know how to handle all of this. You belong to another man. Yes, you might be having a difficult time with him, but the amount of time we spend together here at work will have an effect on you, and I don't want to be a part of any decision you happen to make about your marriage."

Curtis knew that he had to make a decision for the both of them. Because of the way he felt about her he had to be away from her. "Listen, Demetria, I care about you and I always will, but we can't continue to do this."

"But Curtis," Demetria tried to break in.

"No, Demetria, you just listen for a while, okay?"

Demetria became silent. "You have to handle this situation on your own, and while you're doing it, you have to keep everyone else out of it. I'm not sure what your relationship is like with this guy you are married to, but the truth of the matter is, you are married, and I suggest you try and make it work. If you know for a fact that it's not going to work, then get out of it. Don't waste your time or his. Trust me. I have been there and I know the decision is hard, but we only get one chance at life, and you will have to make the right decisions for yourself. There's just not a whole lot left out there. I have been dating now for a few years. Single people all seem to have some type of luggage or ways that they're not willing to let go of. It takes a lot these days for people to just let go and trust that God will provide a mate that will be the one for them."

Demetria just stood there and let Curtis recite his adult's version of the birds and the bees like a preacher man. She could never have prepared for the ton of bricks that came next.

"Demetria, I have made a decision. My department asked me to take a year's salary to resign from my position. They need to roll a few cutbacks, and they are asking for volunteers. I've been debating it for a couple of weeks now, but it seems I have decided to take them up on it."

Demetria gasped. "Curtis, don't do this because of what happened to us. I never intended on hurting you, and I think it would be a mistake to try and run from our friendship," she said.

"Demetria, I'm not running from our relationship. I just need a freaking break from everything. I have the chance to collect a paycheck for a year. My kids are now adults. Don't you see? I wouldn't have any other responsibilities. Anyway, so much has happened here at this damned job. I just need to get the hell away. Please understand that this isn't about you—it's about me."

Demetria didn't say a word, because she probably would have done the same thing given the opportunity. Curtis added, "We will always be in touch. I want you to sort out your business first."

"When is your last day?" Demetria asked.

"I have until the end of the week before I have to clean out my desk."

"Wow, that quick?"

"Well, you know how corporate is. Once they decide to let you go, it doesn't take long to wave you off. Here today, gone tomorrow."

Demetria reached out and hugged Curtis, a tear falling from her eyes.

"I will miss you, Curtis."

"Ditto," he responded.

37

The Last Day

〖▨▨▨〗

C urtis packed up his desk. Reflections of the past five years of his life rolled in and out of his head. The pictures from his wall stared back at him from the box. Each picture served up a portion of the life he had spent at this job. He realized now how much the corporate environment had changed him. Everything he had done since splitting with Grace, he now realized, had been done for survival. He had lost the ability to truly love or be loved. He thought all the way back to the first relationship, the one that sent tremors through his marriage. Whatever happened? He thought he cared enough about this woman to cheat on his wife. Then, he found a reason to push her away. He preyed upon her weaknesses, knowing how long she had been alone. He had manipulated her, he could say now. He had given her reason for suspicion, and then he sat back and waited for her emotions to turn her into a monster, an outrageous foolish monster, so that he could end it with her with no sense of guilt. Curtis looked at the picture of him dancing on the bar. He had to admit it at last.

Then came the second. Curtis knew going in that he would never fall completely for a married woman. There were, first and foremost, in both of their minds, the moral bounds. No matter how close they could get, she was going to put her family first. The pride of any married woman comes down to her family, and Curtis, anyway, would have lost all respect for her if she had left her family for a fantasy life with him or anyone else. He understood her need for a forbidden affair. Maybe one day she would leave her husband, but he had never wanted to be the reason or the destination. It was a fling and nothing more. Curtis knew deep down that their relationship was ephemeral.

Finally, in came Demetria, the woman he would have likely married if he had taken her to bed. But not all women are the marrying kind, especially if you're already proposing from one knee in your head, just looking at her. Curtis knew that he didn't deserve to have a woman like Demetria. Not yet anyway. He still had to redeem all the selfish acts. He still had to suffer for what he had done to Grace. To become happy go lucky, kick around at stones, and try to find happiness just didn't seem right.

Devan had had more of a chance to be with him than anyone else. They had both lived a lot of their lives and made mistakes already. They both were ready to settle down and live life to the fullest. If Devan had just given him time to find himself rather than categorizing him with the other guys who had hurt her before. When Curtis sat down and thought about these women who could have been a part of his life, he imagined growing sad. He had allowed them to think that he was their knight in shining armor. He had wooed them with the notion of marriage. Meanwhile he was just getting to the next day. In the end, he'd left them all behind. Through it all he could never forget about Grace. He dreamed of her everynight. These dreams would come out of thin air. How could she still be very much a part of his life? Altough he had not seen her in some time now, she would come to him everynight. Curtis sometimes hated to awaken from his slumber, knowing that reality would again set in and the ache in his heart would take over. The dreams seemed were more real for him than reality.

38

The Final Confrontation

emetria was the last straw. Curtis was taking an extended vacation. He was tired of all the shit that he had been through. He just wanted to get away. Figuring on a nice and absolute hiatus, he went on a road trip. He had friends he had not seen in years. He wouldn't have to worry about money. It would be time all for Curtis.

His best friend was in Atlanta. He would love a week in New York. Then there was Las Vegas, though he hated losing money senselessly at a casino. After about a month, Curtis made it back home and updated his resume. He needed to put himself back on the market. Luckily, the job was in high demand. This eased Curtis's mind about finding work. Still drawing a salary from his previous position, Curtis took a few more months to decide where he would go next. He considered going back out on the field, but he had gotten used to dressing up, to temperature-controlled atmospheres, consistent hours and oh yeah, the honeys. He had definitely gotten used to the wall-to-wall honeys. They were what got him into trouble in the first place, but damn how he had enjoyed their trouble.

It came down to two companies. One was in the business sector of a home improvements giant. Everything was perfect except for the pay. They wanted to start him off at $10,000 less than the other. There was the possibility of a significant increase within a year based on performance, but $10,000 was $10,000. The other choice was similar to what he had been doing previously. There was a lot more responsibility along with the chance to hop right into management. After a little soul searching, Curtis took the job with higher pay despite his heart that pined for the other. The deciding factor had been the opportunity to get into management. He knew that between bonuses and stock options, he'd make more than he could hope to at the other position.

The interview process was intense. He had five interviews. Once accepted, he started classes that lasted another month. He got more training in his first month at this new company than in all the five years he'd worked before. Training classes were held off site of the main campus, so for the first weeks, he still had not seen any employees other than the new draftees from class. One day Curtis and another one of the new hires decided to have lunch on the main campus at their café, just to check out the food.

The place was nice. The aroma of fresh coffee was in the air, and unlike in a lot of cafés, the cooks were all hidden from sight. There were wooden bookracks with the latest periodicals as well as three televisions, each with distinct programming. Curtis liked the idea of the sofas alongside the tables and chairs. Someone actually put some thought into the layout and design of the cafeteria. It was user friendly. He thought it special and rare that a company would put the comfort of their employees ahead of cutting costs. This new cafeteria was a place you'd actually want to come and relax in.

Curtis especially sought the reading room for solace. This room was partitioned off from the rest of the café with a glass barrier. You could see people on the other side, but the walls were sound proof. You could read, do homework, or just think. It was his new think tank. He started going in there to read a novel he had recently purchased. He loved science fiction and had the new Dean Koontz with him. The book dealt with the creation of humanoids who were human in every way except in their inability to care about others of their kind. These new creatures happened to base all actions on surviving. No matter what had to be done, the objective was survival. In the end, the race of humanoids destroyed each other. They could not trust each other, so they killed each other. Curtis felt that he had somehow turned into a byproduct of this book. Hadn't he been leading his life only to survive?

As he rose to his feet, he heard someone say, "A penny for your thoughts."

The voice was as familiar to him as his own. He hadn't seen her for so long. He had never expected to see her again. Curtis responded, "How much time do you have?"

She smiled her femme fatale smile and motioned for him to sit down. The feeling of disappointment had not completely died in him. Looking at her face again brought a jolt to his heart. He recalled vividly the secrets and lies.

He would not hold it against her. She seemed a different woman, this woman standing before him, this woman who might have risen from her own ashes. An aura of peace was woven into her every expression. Curtis tried to stay calm and collected. He couldn't fall head over heels again, not at the first reunion anyway. The longer they sat and talked though, the more Curtis felt he was being teased and prodded. He would never forget the day she walked out of his house. Her confession trailed behind her like confetti from the piñata she had broken over his head. Emotional rejection was one thing, but sexual rejection on top of it—he remembered sitting on the floor still and dejected as the evening came.

Curtis wanted to get back to work. To repair things was more than they could do in the moments of a workday break. She had broken something inside of Curtis and he didn't want to remember anymore. He had to credit her with that much. Nevertheless, he loosened his tied in disquietude.

Before Curtis could get back to work, she sent him an instant message minutes after he arrived at his desk.

Demetria: It was really good seeing you again, and I would like to make a confession.

Curtis: Yeah, I really enjoyed seeing you as well, and like always, you look great.

Demetria: I just wanted to let you know that I think you are a very handsome young man, and I value your friendship more than you will ever know.

Curtis: That's a confession? I thought you said you had a confession. We never really got to know each other although I think you are a wonderful person too. Anyway, thanks for the compliment. I'm signing off.

Curtis knew women better. This was bait, wasn't it? Well, he thought, she'd have to do better than that. He wasn't biting for such a little morsel.

So she went and texted him.

Demetria: Well, to be quite honest with you, I had a serious crush on you the moment we met. Only because of my situation did I not act on it.

Now this was what Curtis wanted to hear. Now it was on. She had just opened the gates to the kind of conversation he was hoping for.

Curtis: So you're saying that you are not married anymore?

Demetria: I don't want to talk about this on company time. Can we meet tomorrow?

Curtis: I will be on the baseball field all day, but you are welcomed to come out and visit. We can talk afterward.

Demetria: Oh, you play baseball?

Curtis: No, I coach.

Demetria: Okay, I'll call you on this number if I can't make it. If I can, I'll see you then.

Curtis: Talk to you later.

Curtis didn't know what to think. It was all too dizzying. He hid his phone and buried his head in the day's reports.

39

The First Night

E verything went incredibly wrong the day of the game. Not only was Curtis the coach, but he took care of providing for the concession stand. This meant he had to get to the field before everyone else and set up the booths. When Curtis arrived with his job keys instead of the field gate keys, he knew he was headed for a long day. Going back home for the keys would make him late, but he had no other choice. He was one of the two people with keys, and the league president was not expected until later in the morning.

By the time he returned, the players had started arriving and were waiting outside for him to unlock. Curtis made his apologies as he dashed across the small crowd.

"Late night?" someone asked.

The voice was familiar to Curtis. He turned and saw Joan. She was a big flirt, that Joan. She was one of the first buzzards to land when Curtis began his divorce proceedings.

Curtis couldn't respond to Joan. She didn't appeal to him. And if he smiled at her, it was to be polite. Joan, however, loaded his benign smiles with a lot more meaning. She pushed him continually for more than a smile, so Curtis was used to it.

Now they were all late. Everyone rushed to work. Curtis knew hundreds of parents and friends would show up today. He prepared the concessions without his volunteer, who called to say she'd be late. He still had to pick up the few players whose parents didn't have transportation. As he dashed to his car, he could see the flat tire before he got to there. Slapping his forehead, Curtis blurted, "Damn, what else can go wrong?" He realized then that the spare was at home. "That's what can go wrong," he muttered.

He had taken the spare out to make room for the ice cooler. Usually, he would have returned it to the trunk the next day, but the one time he hadn't, there she was, a flat tire.

Curtis rushed over to Joan and asked to borrow her car. Just as he figured, she threw him the keys without hesitation. "You know you owe me, right?"

Curtis thought, "Oh great," but yelled, "I got you."

"Nothing is ever free anymore," Curtis said to himself. Joan wouldn't let him forget, that was for sure. He'd deal with it later though. Curtis rounded up the three boys he had to pick up and made it back to field in record time. If he had picked up the spare, he might have been able to pat himself on the back. As it was, he'd be stuck borrowing from Joan again.

While Curtis was getting the kids ready to play, he received a call from Demetria. She wanted to come and watch him coach. He hoped she would turn his luck around. At least, he would be happier seeing her around. She had never been to the baseball field, so Curtis gave her brief directions and informed her to call when she was close. He assumed she would show.

The game started, and there were still no sign of Demetria. Curtis had already made several coaching mistakes. He was glancing too often at the phone. He knew he was distracted. He kept looking in the direction of the parking lot to see if she had found the park on her own. As the game went on, he was more and more irritated. What a day. Before long the game was out of control. His team was losing by six runs in the bottom of the seventh.

And whose fault was this? Curtis could blame himself for the failings of his team. His mind was somewhere else. He took deep breaths and tried stretching a bit. Curtis decided for his team's sake, he would allow the assistant coach to take over. He watched from the bench as their team lost the next two innings. When the game was over, he gave his players the kind of pep talk expected when you've just got your ass handed to you. He felt like collapsing once tucked behind the safety of the concession stand.

Everything was surprisingly in order. Finally, there was a bright spot to the day. He'd hardly a minute to savor the thought before Joan arrived asking for help. Joan had counted on working with him throughout the day and on collecting for the favor of loaning her car. She knew Curtis wouldn't say no.

"Of course I will help you," Curtis said. "How can I refuse?"

Curtis wasn't looking forward to the next hour side by side with Joan, but at least she would drive him back to his place for the spare.

They were pulling up the drive when she turned to him and said, "So I guess you're not going to invite me in and take advantage of me, huh?"

"Man, I'm so tired, if I wanted to I couldn't tonight," Curtis answered.

What he really wanted to say was "not in a million years," but diplomacy was the best way out today. Curtis got back in her car, they headed back to the field, and he was fixing the tire when his phone rang.

"Hello, how are you?" Demetria said.

Curtis's demeanor changed, and Joan noticed the sudden uplift. She knew Curtis was wooing someone. She just didn't know whom, and she didn't know if she could prevent it from happening. At least, she could have her fun while he was available, Joan thought.

"I'm okay," said Curtis. "Just changing my tire and getting ready to go home. What's up?"

"Well, I was hoping to hear from you tonight, but after you didn't call, I decided to call you."

"Well, I thought I would see you today, but I guess you couldn't make it."

"Yeah, one thing led to another, and before I knew it, the day was gone."

Curtis was, against his will, becoming used to the disappointment. If he didn't expect anything, would he be better off? He hung up the phone, having mumbled yes to her request that he call her after changing the tire.

"Listen, Curtis, I know you have it bad for this girl, but there are obviously some issues here." She paused. "You know I like you, and I'm not looking for a serious connection, but do you think it would be possible for us to go out some time? Maybe you might find out that I'm really not a bad person."

Curtis had known that this conversation would take place sooner or later. He had hoped for later, but here it was, right between the eyes. "Joan, I never said or thought of you as a bad person, but you are right. I do have it bad for Demetria. It wouldn't be fair to start anything with anyone. We can have dinner sometime, as long as you're aware of the situation."

"Well, what is the situation? I have no idea what's going on with you," Joan said.

Curtis didn't want to divulge any more information than necessary. Hell, how could you tell people that you were in love with a married woman, that she has promised you that she will be with you someday? The last thing he wanted was to be caught up with somebody else's somebody. It was too embarrassing now, and he did not want to share it with Joan. Curtis just shook his head and said, "This isn't the best time to talk, but thanks for helping me with my car."

"No problem," Joan said. "I guess I will see you at the meeting on Monday."

"Yeah, see you then."

Curtis couldn't wait to get into his car and call Demetria back. One disappointment after another, and yet, he was locked in more than ever. All he wanted to do was talk to her. The phone rang six times, and Curtis thought she had gone home for the evening, but just before he hung up, Demetria picked up.

"Hello, Curtis, did you get your tire fixed?"

"Yeah, I'm back on the road again. How is it possible for us to be talking tonight?"

Demetria answered, "I just needed to talk to you, so I made it happen. Where are you?"

"I'm just leaving the field and on my way home," Curtis said.

"Going out tonight?" Demetria asked.

"No, I'm going home and will probably go to bed. Why are you asking me these questions? Are you going out tonight?" Curtis asked.

"No, I don't think so, but who knows?"

"Wait a minute," Curtis said. "Where are you?"

"I'm riding around in your neighborhood waiting on you to come home," she said.

As Curtis was talking to Demetria, he wasn't paying attention to the fact that his car was veering off the road. As oncoming traffic starting blowing their horns, Curtis nearly drove off the road and into a tree. "Wait a minute. Where did you say you were?"

"What are you, hard of hearing? I'm about five minutes away from your house. How long will it take to get your butt here?"

"Hell, I will be there in five minutes. Go ahead and go in. There is an extra key under the mat." Curtis always kept a key there just for these type situations.

"You must have known I was coming?" she asked.

"No, I keep that there for my mom. She likes to come over and clean sometimes when I'm working."

"Whatever," Demetria said. "I will be here when you get home."

The smile on Curtis's face was so big, he must have appeared crazy to everybody who saw him. Her voice rang through his world. Curtis kept hearing, "I'm waiting on you to come home." He truly wished that there'd be a day he'd come home always to the same sentence. "I'm waiting on you to come home." This was one sentence that Curtis could hear daily.

Curtis arrived and saw Demetria's car already parked in the drive. He gushed in excitement and hoped the house had been clean for her. He hadn't expected anyone over, and least of all, her. When he walked in, a candle was burning in the living room. The lights were low. Demetria was lying on the couch with his bed pillows.

"So how are you, young man?" Demetria asked.

"I'm doing better now that I am home," he said. "And with you here, couldn't get any better."

"I took the liberty of running your bath water for you. I hope you don't mind. I figured after a long day you might want to relax a little."

"You were being very kind," he said, playing the part. "Only you must join me. That would make me very happy."

"Maybe I will," she said. "But you go ahead while I fix us a drink."

Curtis couldn't believe that he was going to be in the same tub as Demetria! How on earth had this happened, and what could he do to keep it from ending? He couldn't have planned it or wished it or pulled it from a rose petal sky. He was in the bubble-soaked tub when Demetria came in carrying two glasses of Merlot.

"Wow, thanks, Demetria. You must have read my mind. This is just what I needed."

"Yeah, I kinda figured that. You have been running since early today. Now it's time for you to relax." She handed Curtis his drink. He reached out for her other hand and kissed her lightly on the lips.

"That was nice," she said, pressing her lips in for a more urgent and passionate kiss. Curtis realized that he had started to have a reaction to her touch. He appreciated every bubble in the tub. He started to push Demetria away before she would notice.

"Don't be shy," Demetria said. "I seen it long before you pushed me away." The devilish grin, he remembered well.

"I knew the possibility of it before I kissed you," she said.

By now Curtis had a full erection. He reached over and put a washcloth to cover himself. "Are you getting in or what?" he asked.

"No, I'm not. I never told you I was getting in the tub with you. What I said was I would join you in the bathroom. I came to keep you company, if you don't mind."

Here was disappointment again. "I guess I just made an ass of myself assuming you were getting in here with me."

Demetria laughed. She knew her power. She knew he wasn't to blame for being misled. "I'm sorry, Curtis. I have already taken a bath, and I'm as fresh as a daisy."

Curtis lathered his washcloth and started to scrub. "You're serious then, that you are going to sit there and watch me take a bath? The least you can do is wash my back," Curtis said.

"Are you sure it's safe? The last time I touched you, you had to cover up."

"I think my back is more immune. Yeah, go on. My back is safe. Here," Curtis said, handing her the washcloth.

She started with small circular motions. Top to bottom. Then she worked on his butt cheeks. "Is this safe?" she asked.

"Don't know, what do you think?" Curtis responded.

Demetria reached around and touched Curtis from the front. It was so easy. He was fully erect. "I guess nowhere is safe on your body, huh?"

Curtis laughed and said, "It has been that way since I touched you the first time. It doesn't even require touch. Your presence is enough. Just your presence."

Demetria pushed him away and said she wanted to see what kind of music he had. "I'll be out there soon," Curtis said. "Just make yourself at home."

Demetria looked over her shoulder at him. "Don't worry. I will."

Curtis finished bathing and heard one of his old CDs playing. It was Randy Brown. Demetria recognized the name but couldn't remember why. As she played the album, she suddenly remembered why the name was familiar. The song was one of her favorite songs when she was a young girl.

"Where did you dig this up? I haven't heard this since high school."

"I didn't have to dig it up. I have had this since it came out. I have been a Randy Brown fan for a long time."

"Some songs are just ageless," Demetria said, sighing. "And this is one of those songs."

Curtis had been on the run all day. He was exhausted, but he stayed up all night talking to Demetria. Before they knew it, the sun was rising. They went into the bedroom and got into bed. Curtis wanted to make love to her so badly. Instead, he wrapped his arms around her and fell asleep.

40
Making Love to Demetria

urtis lay in bed under the magnificent blue illumined fish tank lights and thought happily of Demetria. He was desperately falling in love again. She seemed to fill every part of his consciousness. All he could think was how much he thought Demetria was different from any other woman he had met. She had this charisma they Curtis adored. It was the first time that he had escaped the past, the dead marriage, the courtships that had resulted in sex and self-sabotage. Curtis smiled tenderly, confident that he was finally ready to move on with his life, to fall in love, to forget about everything else. He believed that Demetria loved him just as deeply—even if for the time being, she was a married woman and it might be months before they could begin a normal relationship.

Curtis's advice to his children had always been, believe 20 percent in a person's words and 80 percent in thier actions. Even as he dreamed, the old doubting voices came in. "Why don't you follow your own rules, Curtis?"

Demetria always said the right things, but how often did her actions actually match her words? Rather, she'd broken promise after promise as Curtis accepted apology after apology. Days, weeks, and even months had been stalled for the sake of appeasing, letting her run the dysfunctional relationship she seemed to have with her husband. When it didn't completely halt Curtis's life, it certainly stunted it. He would put off making any plans because Demetria might free up some time here or there or at the last minute. He lived in vain, waiting on her, night and day, and that early taint of disappointment he'd felt was never quite quelled. He knew also that the worst was ahead of them. Divorce could lick up the best intentions. He could not put his finger on it, but there was something dishonest in all of it. Had she revealed her innermost truths? Or was she just a woman looking for excitement? Now that Curtis was ready to make a serious connection, it was not possible anymore to do so with Demetria holding all the cards. She told Curtis that she was fed up with her husband, but then, there would be long days that he would not hear any more from her. He was sure she was spending time with him and not picking up the phone, but was it possible for Curtis to be wrongfully upset and jealous that she was making up with her husband. On the nights they were not talking on the phone, was she lying in his arms?

Could Curtis really believe that she was no longer sleeping with her husband, that she felt compelled to continue the marriage if in name only? It seemed improbable to him that a man and woman could live under the same roof without talking or having sex. If Curtis were to trust his instincts, he'd say that even the way she answered the phone while at home was strained. Was this just another form of punishment, another act of redemption after what he'd done to Grace? That affliction, Grace's unconscious but great karmic revenge—was it not his destiny to suffer as he had made her suffer? The more he tried to control and shelter his heart, the more it was ripped piece by piece. And what could he do about it?

Curtis allowed Janice to fall in love with him knowing that he would never reciprocate. One after the other, he had forged walls that were paper-thin and constructed of whimsy. This was payback. For Demetria to plunge him down the same isolated path seemed logical to him. Demetria needed an out, and Curtis was there to give her one just as Janice had been there for him.

Curtis turned on the bed, agitated and lonely. He remembered making love to Demetria. It was the night after a long phone conversation that twisted and turned for hours and was comprised of news, children, and other niceties. It was a time when her husband was out of town on business. For whatever reason though, instead of hanging up, they stayed on the line and allowed something that was now at once relentless and unresisting between them take over.

Curtis asked Demetria what she was wearing. "At the moment I still have on the same outfit I wore today. I haven't hopped in the shower yet," she answered.

"So when are you going to take a shower?" Curtis asked.

"The moment we hang up. I'm going to soak for about an hour," she said.

"Damn, I wish I could be there to wash your back for you and maybe your legs or your arms or anything else that might need washing," Curtis said.

"Are you telling me that you are willing to bathe me as if I was your little girl?"

"I will bathe you as if you were my wife," Curtis said excitedly. "I will wash every part of your body, maybe even twice. I will then dry you off inch by inch, pick you up, and lay you down in bed."

Demetria listened in attentive rapture. "What will you do to me after that?" she asked.

That was the opening Curtis had been looking for. He and Demetria had never talked about sex before. He thought it was a subject long overdue. They had talked about god, children, family, the ways to grill corn, you name it—they'd touched on it. "I don't think you are ready for what I might do to you after. I would hate for you to become an addict of my touch."

"I think I'm old enough to decide what habits I would like to start," Demetria said.

"I have been craving your touch for so long. I just want to take you in my arms and make love to you all night. I want you to feel me inside of you.

Hearing the words made the hairs on Demetria's neck rise. She was already in an extremely sexy mood. She was always extremely aroused in the days prior to her menstrual cycle and it was due to come on in a few days. She gasped at the thought of having more than one orgasm. She knew she needed to see Curtis.

"You sure talk a lot of trash for someone who is forty-five minutes away," Demetria said.

What was she doing, he wondered. It was three in the morning, and she was trying to coax him out of home and bed. "Don't tempt me, Demetria. You know I will be on my way in two minutes, can be there in forty-seven."

"So what's taking you so long? You should be in the car by now," Demetria teased. The invitation was her inevitable plunge. She was so stimulated by now; she probably would have gotten out of bed and gone to his house if it came down to that. Now all she had to do was to wait. Curtis was already in his car and on the way. He was just as provoked.

"I will call you when I am entering your complex," Curtis said.

"I will leave the door open," she said.

Demetria was also having last minute jitters. This first impression was going to go a long way and last them till the end. Oh, why was she saying "end." This was just the beginning. She took a long shower and lathered up her Victoria's Secret soaps. She piled on the scents of lotion and posed this way and that on the bed. He was coming to her.

Curtis came in without a sound and followed the trail of scent to her room. He could feel himself already quite erect. How long had he dreamed of this moment? He had never seen a more beautiful woman. Had he wanted to say a mouthful of promises, he would have failed. The only sound that came to his lips was an utterance and hardly that. "Damn," he said.

Curtis told himself he was a lucky man as he walked toward Demetria. There he was, about to make love to the woman of his dreams. She looked ravishing stretched out upon the bed. He felt the palms of his hands slippery with anticipation and nervousness. He approached, put a finger on her leg, and lightly kissed her lips.

"You smell so good. What are you wearing?" Curtis asked.

"I'm not sure, just something I have from a long time ago."

"You, Demetria, are exquisite," Curtis said.

Demetria smiled as she lured Curtis's head gently to her chest as though she were cradling a baby. He sank right into her arms and positioned himself on top of her. They lay there for a moment, close and snug, each of them wondering what would follow. "Will you be okay?" Curtis asked.

Demetria kissed him in response. Curtis pulled away and took one more look before he started to undress her. Demetria had a sheer top on that tied in the middle and a pair of boy shorts that matched. Curtis pulled the string, and her top fell off her shoulders. She had a perfect pair of breasts. Curtis couldn't wait to get his mouth around them. As he lowered his head to kiss her breasts, Demetria dug her fingers into the back of his hair and pressed his head tightly to her. Curtis took her breasts into his mouth and sucked on them as he played with her nipple with the tip of his tongue. Demetria was so hot she could almost feel Curtis entering her. She started to move her pelvis, and Curtis realized that this was really going to happen.

Curtis reached down, grabbed Demetria's hand, and placed it on his penis so she could feel what she was doing to him. She rubbed her hand up and down the shaft of Curtis's penis as he caressed her vagina through the boy shorts. He could feel the moistness through the underwear. The only worthwhile thing left was to kiss her down there. As he lowered his head, she grabbed him by the ear and said, "What are you doing, Curtis?"

"Don't stop me, Demetria. Just lie back and relax," Curtis said. At his destination, Curtis kissed her in all her places. She began to turn, squeal, and gyrate uncontrollably. She moaned and moaned with her hips high in the air. Curtis looked up at the expression on her face and smiled. Regardless of what happened now, he knew she'd already been satisfied. Nothing ever pleased him more than the cry of a woman's orgasm.

Demetria pulled him up and looked into his eyes. "You did that on purpose, didn't you?"

"Of course," Curtis replied. "Did you enjoy it?"

Demetria stared at him as she bent his penis into her. Curtis was now deep in her and feeling surreal. He climaxed but continued to stroke Demetria. He felt as if he could go on forever. The second time would be even more of a rush. Curtis found himself letting out a moan similar to the one that came from Demetria. They were both sweating. He had sweat dripping down his face onto her belly and hips. Demetria started blowing on Curtis to try to cool him off.

"Damn, that feels good, Demetria," Curtis said.

Curtis's arms went limp, and he lowered himself beneath her. He rolled over and cradled her from behind. They slept until sunrise.

41
Out of Control

I n the days after Curtis and Demetria made love, a void grew between them. Curtis would call, and she would not return his calls. He decided that he would send her an e-mail to see if would get a response:

Hello Baby,

This letter is the result of another restless night that I am experiencing continually thinking of you. I need to write this in order to let you know some things that may be a little difficult to say. Dreams of you have begun to consume all my waking hours. But there is something going on with you that I feel you are not telling. I know you are having issues with your husband, and I have come to two different conclusions:

1) You are sincere in your conversations with me and are really struggling to spare the feelings of someone whom you care for dearly. In this case, I truly sympathize with you because this will be no easy task. There is never an easy way to say good-bye. You know how I feel about you, but I advise you as I would my own daughter. If you are honest with yourself, you know that I am right. I have tried not to say anything negative about your significant other since you explicitly said you didn't want to hear any bashing. It's too hard though to suppress what I feel about you.

2) You are really on an emotional rollercoaster and are not sure of what you really want. In this case, you need to be honest with everyone involved. I have learned that emotions are nothing to play with. Please be aware of everyone in your circle and what things they may be capable of. I would rather you tell me that you are struggling with your decision so that I may have the option to continue on my path or just chill until you are definite about your intentions.

I want you to realize, Demetria, how real my feelings are for you. I think it is best that we stop where we are and not continue until you're sure of what you want. I value my feelings, and I refuse to let them get out of control. Yet I've gotten tangled in a situation where I can only be the bad guy. I will continue to help you as I promised, but I can't continue to let my feelings for you get any stronger. I will always know that you are the love of my life. If we are meant to be, it will happen. I love you enough to let you go. This action may fall under the category that states nice guys finish last, but if in this case it is true, so be it.

Curtis didn't hear from Demetria. He decided he'd write to her personal e-mail address.

Hey Demetria,

Here I go again. I hope you are having and/or will have a productive day. I was in the neighborhood and decided to drop off a token of my affection for you. I know you also wanted these other items as well. Please know that you are the most important person I've ever known and will ever know. I have met a lot of people in my forty-two years, and I have never found one like you. Please realize that whatever I have to endure to be with you, I am willing. I have never told you, but I feel that we are truly soul mates. I wish that we could have met before, but I have to believe that this may be the time that was destined for us, as rocky as it may seem. Life can bring about the unexpected. I thought losing my daughter or divorcing my family was the most difficult thing that I would ever experience. I was wrong. Being in love with someone and not being able to be with that person is far more difficult. When I met you at Dracoa, I fell for the Demetria I knew then, but I didn't think you would ever be within my reach. Now that I have a chance to have you in my life, my emotions are overwhelming me. I am getting ready to leave the house for dinner, but I had to write this letter. I hope that you continue to be the person that I fell in love with. Whatever you do, don't be afraid of what we can have together. We can reach the stars together. I love you more than life itself. I have never appreciated this cliché until I met you.

Finally, Demetria replied. She wanted to meet for lunch. She wrote in a flat and dry tone, which made Curtis concerned.

42

The Signs Were There

urtis waited ten minutes before he decided to go on to lunch without Demetria. He really thought she was coming this time. He never expected anything from her, but still, it was disappointing whenever she didn't do what she'd volunteered to do. Curtis never understood. He was always on time. If he said he would do something, you could best believe it would be done. Demetria had pulled this before, and it was starting to get old. Curtis decided that he wouldn't call this time to get an explanation. He would just see how long it would take her to call, what excuse she would offer.

Curtis's three o'clock break came and went, and still he'd had no word from Demetria. Accustomed to married women, he spent the time wondering what had happened to keep her. Was it possible that they had reconciled, that he'd be left out in the dark? He was really in love with Demetria though. She had done something to him. He couldn't shake it no matter how he tried. Before he knew it, he had logged onto his Yahoo account and written her an e-mail. He was steadfast about not calling, but he wanted to put his thoughts on record, so he wrote:

Hello Demetria,

I am going to try to pay a little more attention to myself. I can thank you for the advice. Lately I have lost more and more control, and I have never lived like that. I was careful not to become too wrapped up in something that would alter the person that I am, but our situation is causing a reaction in other aspects of my life that I hadn't expected. I'll give you examples. Yesterday, I had to put in the same purchase order three times because I couldn't concentrate long enough to complete it without making mistakes.

It's all the little things, and while I know you are going through a difficult time, I am quite sure that my being intertwined in your problems has made me mentally inept. I have taken your problems for my own. To make things worse, I can't even seem to see you as much as I'd like. It feels like I'm doing something wrong. It really does. I'm beginning to question my own motives, as sincere as I know them to be. I love you and want to live my life letting you know this, but I can't continue torturing myself. I truly think that you are being mentally tortured, which means that same thing is happening to me. Every time I check your text message, it seems as though I am playing a form of Russian Roulette, and I'm just waiting around until you finally drop the axe. Maybe this is another one of those cases where I am over-thinking, but you try to put yourself in my place. Imagine my being married, living with someone, and that person is doing everything in her power to keep me there, and I am falling for it. It wouldn't matter what was said or who was saying it. The conclusions are your own to form. The text I sent to you was more than just frustration. I sent you a text one night and said I wanted to talk to you. Well, this is the conversation I wanted to have. There is no question about how I feel. You know that. It's just this rollercoaster is starting to get the best of me. You have to make up your mind whether or not you want to leave your husband, and I can't help you with that. There are a lot of things that I am capable of doing, but that isn't one of them. Unlike him, I love you enough to let go. I am willing to concede to him. If you decide to let him get his own place, I guess everything I said in this letter would be in vain. But I'm guessing he has found a way to let you give him a few more days to find a place to live. I hope I am wrong about everything I am feeling right now, but che serà serà.

Once Curtis sent the e-mail he knew that if she really loved him she would respond. Maybe he had been wrong about her the entire time. Who knew anymore? Curtis had always heard about women who would do anything to achieve certain goals. Did she keep Curtis around to make her husband jealous? Was this a ploy to let her husband know that there were quality men out eager and willing to have and to hold her?

Curtis remembered that he had used Janice to get away from his married life. Could Demetria be working the same agenda? Or did she really love Curtis and she was struggling with the decision to cut ties with him? Regardless of her reasoning, Curtis was injured, and the little faith in people that he held on to would diminish if what he thought he had with Demetria had been all a lie. How could she be so convincing to make him think that she too was falling in love?

Demetria used to tell Curtis how manipulative her husband was. Maybe she learned how to be just as calculating. As far as Curtis was concerned, maybe they planned it all together.

But why would she let Curtis fall in love like that? He had never asked her for anything. He had always told her that he wasn't helping to receive anything from her, that he truly wanted to help her as a friend. Maybe Demetria was a real life *Desperate Housewife* looking for attention. Maybe that was what the affair meant to her. All he wanted to do was get a reply that would explain it all to him.

Curtis waited for days and didn't hear from Demetria. He decided to call her, and to his surprise her husband answered her phone. Curtis didn't say anything. He just hung up. Now, he knew it had all been a lie.

Physically Curtis felt like shit. He called in sick for a week. He didn't even want to come to work anymore. He called his job and told them he was done. He wasn't coming back to work. Curtis had saved enough money to live on for a couple of years. After this shattering blow, he just wanted to be alone and not talk to anyone. After a few more days and no response from Demetria, he started to become angry. He had to know what was going on. As far as he knew, Demetria's husband could be holding her hostage or something; his imagination was starting to get the best of him. Curtis decided that he would ride by her house to see if he could get a glimpse of something to help him close this door.

He borrowed Darnell's car to protect his identity. No one was around. The house looked vacant to him. Although the grass had been cut, it was brown and withered. Demetria lived in a small community on the outskirts of town where they were strict about the appearance of the houses. The community maintained the lawn, but the occupants were responsible for the upkeep. It was obvious that the yard hadn't been watered all summer.

Curtis decided that he wasn't going to leave until he'd seen her. She had to come out eventually. Curtis picked an inconspicuous place and camped out. He knew that if he parked there long enough, the security guard would eventually approach the car. After about an hour, the garage door opened, and Demetria's car backed out of the drive. Curtis lowered his head.

Curtis picked up the phone and tried to call her. She wouldn't answer. Why wasn't she answering his calls? He was determined to know. He followed her until she stopped for gas. Curtis didn't approach yet. He wanted to see where she was going, and the gas station was too close to her house. Demetria finished pumping gas and started driving again. After a few more minutes, she pulled into a shopping center and went grocery shopping. Curtis realized that she might head back home when she left the store, so he decided to go in. He grabbed a shopping cart and walked around until he bumped into her.

"Demetria!" Curtis called.

She was startled at first, and then she seemed really frightened. "What are you doing here, Curtis?" she asked.

"What in the hell did you expect me to do? I have been trying to contact you for weeks. I didn't know what to think."

"Well, I'm okay," Demetria explained. "You shouldn't be here."

"I know that, but I need some answers, and I'm not going home until you tell me something."

"I can't do this here, not now," Demetria said.

"So what do you want me to do?"

"When I leave here, I have to go to my mother's house and take her a few things. Meet me there, and I will explain what's going on."

Curtis said okay and waited outside until he'd watched her leave. He followed her to her mom's place and waited down the street until she came back out. She still hadn't noticed that he was in someone else's car. She looked up and down the road as though he hadn't come. As she went to get in her car, Curtis blew the horn and flashed his high beams. Demetria walked over to the car.

"Whose car are you in, and why are you following me?"

"Hop in, Demetria. We need to talk."

"I don't know if that will be a good idea, Curtis. There is a lot of crazy shit going on, and you are right in the middle of it."

"Demetria, I told you earlier. I am not leaving until we talk." Curtis was adamant about his decision.

"Okay, but I don't have a whole lot of time, and I don't want you to get upset about what I'm going to tell you."

She got in the car, and Curtis started driving. "So tell me," he said.

"He found the letter you wrote to me."

"What letter?"

"The e-mail that we had sent back and fourth, the nipple one."

"How did you let him see that, Demetria?"

"I didn't realize he had guessed my password and had been randomly checking my e-mail for some time now. All before that e-mail, things had been quite innocent, but that e-mail contained things that made it very obvious we had slept together."

"Well, I'm sorry to hear that he read the e-mail, but what does it matter? You were planning on leaving anyway, weren't you?"

"I haven't changed my mind. It's just that things have gotten more complicated. He also showed me a picture of you, Curtis."

"What do you mean, a picture of me?"

"A picture! Evidently he has been having someone follow you. I don't answer the phone because it's bugged. My car too."

"Why do you say that?" Curtis asked.

"Because the last time we were together, he knew. He knew where we were and what we did. I don't want to put you in the middle of this shit, so that's why I have to stay away from you. I love you more than anything in this world, and if anything happened to you, I couldn't live with myself."

"Listen, Demetria, I can take care of myself. You need to be concerned about your own well-being. I don't care about how many pictures of me he has. He will not approach me. I can guarantee you that. Are you frightened for your own safety?" Curtis asked.

"No, I really don't think he will harm me in any kind of way."

"Are you sure, Demetria?"

"Yes, I'm sure. But know that he has this personal vendetta against you. He's said that he will not leave, no matter what. He told me that you've ruined his life."

Curtis was upset now. "Demetria, this is a ploy on his behalf. Why are you falling for this weak ass con game?"

Curtis couldn't understand why she was still there with him. He was convinced that something else was going on. Curtis had been driving for a while now, and he wanted to stop somewhere to continue the conversation. Curtis had automatically driven in the direction of his house. Demetria, when she realized, protested.

"Where are we going Curtis?" she asked.

"I'm going to my house."

"We can't go there," she explained. "Didn't I tell you that he must have some type of tracking system on my car?"

"We aren't in your car," Curtis responded.

Demetria stayed in the car and insisted on talking outside. "I told you that I didn't have that much time," she said.

Curtis reached over and ran his fingers though her hair. He knew this was one of her weaknesses. "I miss you, baby," he said.

"Curtis, I miss you too, but this isn't going to work. Now we came here to talk, so let's stick to that, ok?"

"Listen, Demetria," Curtis started to explain. "When we are not together, I can't think. I am not working anymore because I just don't want to be around anyone. I need you in my life right now. I can't function without you."

Curtis reached over, put his arms around her neck, and brought her closer. He could feel her breathing start to get erratic. He knew that this was a sign of her being turned on or fear. "Why are you trying to seduce me, Curtis? You know we shouldn't be together until I get my life together."

"Demetria, I may never see you again. Life is too uncertain not to take advantage of every opportunity that comes your way. I want to be with you, and I need to feel your body against mine. Come inside with me, just for a moment."

Curtis kissed her passionately on her pouting mouth. Demetria looked into his eyes and couldn't resist any longer. They went inside hand in hand. Soon after, they were both naked in the living room kissing each other. Curtis backed his way into the bedroom and fell on his back. Demetria positioned herself on top of him, and Curtis's penis slid right into place as if it had some sort of tracking device for Demetria's vagina.

They had both needed it. She was just beginning to shed real tears of joy when the doorbell rang. Curtis had this overwhelming feeling of déjà vu. Demetria looked at Curtis and asked if he was expecting anyone. Curtis said that he wasn't, but said that he had an idea that it was her husband.

"What do you mean, you think it's my husband?"

"I don't know, Demetria. I just have this strange feeling that's who is at my door. I don't have people just pop up over here."

Demetria swung her body off Curtis. The doorbell rang again. The person had started to bang on the door. Curtis was now sure that they had been followed or that Demetria was being tracked somehow. Demetria was more and more convinced that Curtis had a point. It could be her husband.

"Please don't tell him I'm here," she said as Curtis walked out. The same words Curtis spoke to Janice years earlier.

"I know," he said.

"Who is it?" Curtis asked, looking out the peephole.

"Just tell my wife to come out."

Curtis opened the door and looked the guy in the face. He said innocently, "Excuse me?"

"Listen, I know you know who I am, and you must also know that I know that she is here," he said. "I just want you to tell her to come on out."

Curtis, shirtless, reached down and purposely zipped up his pants and buttoned them, looked at this man standing in his doorway, and said, "I have no clue who you are, and your wife is not here, but if you are looking for a quick ass kicking you've come to the right place."

"The only thing I want is my wife to come out of there, and if she refuses now, tell her I will deal with her when she gets home."

Curtis smiled and stepped into the man's chest. "I suggest you get your ass in that car and leave before I do something that I will regret tomorrow."

Curtis knew that if he got close enough her husband would smell her perfume. Curtis wanted him to know that she was there, and there was nothing he could do about it.

The man backed up and said as he walked off, "This shit isn't over."

Curtis was certain that this wasn't going to be their last confrontation, but he knew he could take this guy, so it really didn't matter. The only reason he didn't get into his ass then was because he knew Demetria was there, and she wouldn't have wanted it to go down like that. When Curtis went back into the room, Demetria was fully dressed and sitting on the edge of the bed.

"I told you we shouldn't have come here, Curtis. I told you."

Now Curtis was really getting agitated. He had been waiting far too long for Demetria to leave this jerk, and it was either now or never.

"Listen, Demetria, the man knew you were here with me tonight, but I guarantee you that it doesn't change anything with him. He may have a few words with you when you get home, but the fact remains. He is not going to leave that house. He is determined to keep you away from me, and you are letting him continue to manipulate the whole situation. I am not going to go through this anymore with you," Curtis fumed.

"Could you please take me to my car?" Demetria said.

She had never answered Curtis one way or the other, so he decided that he would not ask her any more questions. They spent the ride in silence. She got out of the car and ran over to her own, and never looked back at Curtis. They drove off in their separate directions.

43

Demetria's Plan Finalized

D emetria arrived home and found her husband packing a small suitcase. He stormed into the room the moment he heard her come in. She turned on her television. She'd decided not to run and hide, but to face it head on. Before she could put the remote control down on the nightstand, he was there at her door.

"So where have you been?" he asked.

"Although it's none of your business, I went to the market and to my mother's house," Demetria said.

"Demetria, you don't have to lie to me anymore. I know you were at his house tonight. Why won't you just admit it?"

"Admit what? Admit that you are having me followed and that you may have my car Lojacked too?"

"It doesn't matter how I know. I just know you were over to his house. Now I want to hear you admit it."

"Well, if that's what you are waiting on, you might as well pull up a chair because you will never hear me say that," Demetria said.

"Demetria, I know you went to the store. I know you left there and went to your mom's, and I know he picked you up from there and took you to his house. I don't care if you admit it or not. I've seen this with my own two eyes."

Demetria looked at him in disgust. "You are a pathetic man," she said. "Why are you continuing to embarrass yourself in this way? Our marriage is over, and it has been over for months. I don't want you anymore, and you can't force me to love you again. I have lost all feeling. I wish you would just leave," Demetria said. As harsh as it sounded, it wasn't anything she hadn't said before. He'd still never left.

At least, this time, he wasn't arguing with her. After a torturing silence, he said, "I'm leaving. I just wish you were woman enough to have told me the truth and not run behind my back and sleep with another man."

"I told you the truth a long time ago," Demetria said. "I'm not in love with you anymore, and it's not because of another man. It's because of you."

As her husband walked out of the room with tears in his eyes, it saddened Demetria to know that she was hurting him more than he had ever hurt her before. The only consolation for hurting anyone you've once loved—remembering all the times they've done it to you. She pulled out the box of greeting cards. There were dozens of them, each with the same caption. "I'm sorry, Demetria, for hurting you. It will never happen again."

She got a card every time he screwed up. A card for every time he'd gone gambling, drinking, or sleeping around—most of the time, all three. Demetria remembered going to his mistress's house at three in the morning to prove that he was there, and all he could do was give her greeting cards that said how sorry he was. As she started to rip the cards up, she couldn't help but cry. Her marriage was over, and although it wasn't her fault, she felt as though she had failed in some way. Hearing the front door slam, she looked out of the window and saw her husband throw the last of his items on the back of his truck. He looked up at her, lowered his head, got in his car, and drove away.

Demetria lay down for a few hours. She couldn't believe that he had finally left. She wanted so desperately to call Curtis, but decided to wait a few days. Just as she started to fall asleep, she got a text message:

"Good Night and I love you." It was Curtis. She didn't stop to think twice. She picked up the phone and dialed his number. The phone rang once before Curtis picked it up.

"Hello, Demetria. I see you got my message."

"Yeah, I got it."

"Didn't think I would hear from you so soon."

"Yeah, I know. I just wanted to talk to you, so I picked up the phone and called."

"Demetria, are you home alone?" Curtis asked, since it was 2:00 a.m.

Curtis was playing right into Demetria's plan. She knew that he would realize that she was there by herself and that her husband was gone for good. Curtis asked if he could come over, and although she hesitated, she decided to let him come for a few minutes. When Curtis arrived at the house, Demetria was sitting on the front porch in her nightclothes. Curtis, feeling a little uncomfortable, had parked his car on the opposite street.

Demetria was startled when she saw him. "Where did you come from?" she asked.

"I parked around the corner. I just don't feel right parking in front of your house."

She rose to her feet and gave Curtis a hug. He could feel her body through the sheer nightgown she had on. Demetria was sure now they'd end up in bed. Not a minute passed and the two were making love like there was no tomorrow against the interior of the front door. Before he knew it, Curtis heard the back door of Demetria's house open and slam shut. He didn't have a chance to react before Demetria's husband was coming at him with a crowbar.

"I told your ass that this wasn't over," he said.

Curtis pulled himself away from Demetria and picked up a lamp from the table by the front door. Demetria shrieked, "Please stop. Don't do this." Her cries were unheard.

Curtis and her husband were about to start a battle that she'd orchestrated. When her husband caught her earlier at Curtis's house, she knew that he must have LoJacked Curtis's car and not hers. She also knew that the only thing that would drive her husband to react in a violent way against Curtis was to have him think that Curtis was in his house with her. She knew if she had told Curtis that she was home alone that he would be compelled to come over. Her plan had worked perfectly.

As they fought, Demetria played the enraged wife/mistress like an Emmy-winning actress. Curtis had bought himself enough time by picking up the lamp to regain his composure and was now starting to get the best of his opponent. Demetria knew though that her husband had been pushed to the point of no return. He wasn't going to let Curtis have his wife no matter what he had to do. She wanted her husband dead. The plan was for Curtis to kill him, but the only way Curtis would take it that far was in self-defense. She had to think quickly. And to act. If Curtis was down, her husband wouldn't get the final blow he deserved. She had to close this deal today. Demetria got close enough to let her husband grab her. She knew that he would try to use her to stop Curtis from kicking his ass. He reached out and grabbed Demetria by the ankle. She fell in the direction of the table by the door. She knew that he kept the house gun in the drawer. She opened the drawer and took out the gun. Then she dropped it so her husband could pick it up. Grabbing the gun, he pointed it at Curtis and pulled the trigger. Curtis flinched. The gun had blanks and only clicked. Demetria had taken out the bullets earlier.

"Hit him," Demetria screamed.

Before her husband could pull the trigger again, Curtis hit him with a blow to the head that rendered him unconscious. Curtis rolled over, took the gun out of his hands, and threw it down the hall. As he lay there trying to catch his breath, he realized that Demetria's husband was bleeding excessively.

He crawled to him and checked for a pulse. "I don't feel a pulse," Curtis said.

"What do you mean?" Demetria asked. "See if he's breathing."

"I don't think so," Curtis said.

"Call 911 and hurry," Curtis said, now panicking.

He was already dead when the ambulance came. The police questioned both Demetria and Curtis.

"Who lives here?" Sergeant Houston asked.

"I do," Demetria said, holding her head down and never making eye contact.

Pointing at the body on the floor, the officer asked, "And who is this?"

"That's my ex-husband," Demetria said as she looked away.

"So I guess you must be the boyfriend," the officer said to Curtis.

"No, just a friend," Curtis answered.

"Well Ms...."the officer said.

"Tolbert," Demetria offered.

"Ms. Tolbert, could you please follow me? I need to ask you a few more questions."

He walked her away from the scene. Curtis started to follow them but was told to stay put. The officer wanted to speak to Demetria alone. Curtis started to have a real fucked up feeling in his stomach. He had no idea what she would tell them. For all he knew she would throw him under the bus.

The officer now asked Demetria what happened, and she explained that her ex-husband had come there uninvited and fought with them. He had fired an empty gun at Curtis. She explained that he had a trespassing warrant against him and that she had feared for her life. She described Curtis as a good friend who happened to be there when her ex came over. Her story was precise. She told the officer that when her ex pulled the trigger, Curtis hit him thinking he might pull the trigger again, not knowing that the blow would be fatal. She made Curtis out to be a hero.

The story was too clean for the officer's taste, however. After he talked to Demetria, he asked Curtis a few questions. It was the same story—the story of a dead husband, an ex-wife and her friend who'd acted in self-defense.

44

Déjà vu

H e hadn't heard from Demetria. He found himself staring at the phone for interminable hours waiting for it to ring. Finally, he texted her. "Are we going to talk or what?"

She replied soon after. "I was just texting you. I will meet you in the diner at twelve o'clock."

Curtis went to meet her with a sick sensation. Something was seriously wrong, and he knew it had to do with that night. Curtis did not know what she had done.

She had worked all her life to get to where she was and had decided that she did not want to pay her husband a dime. He had used her the entire time they were married, and she refused to continue to let him do it after the divorce was final. She had observed Curtis when they worked together before and knew that if she made him fall in love, he would love deeply enough to protect her.

Curtis was anxious. He couldn't tell what she'd say or do now. She had promised an explanation for not spending the weekend together. But then, he'd sent her a text telling her an explanation wasn't necessary. He just wanted to know where they stood. It was now after twelve, and she hadn't shown. He decided to go ahead to the diner until he heard from her. He went for Southern food at Henratty's. He always ordered the chicken tender lunch special. The same young server was there. She always waited on him. A petite white girl, no older than twenty-four, she smiled happy to see Curtis.

"What will it be today, Curtis? Are you having the usual?"

"Of course!" Curtis said. He didn't even look at the menu. "Maybe tomorrow, you'll pick something new out for me."

"Yeah right," the server said. Curtis always promised to try something different but never did. "You are stuck on the tenders. I'm not going to try and convert you."

"The only thing I am stuck on is you being such a good hostess. If you weren't here, those tenders would not be as nearly so good. I don't think I'd even be able to come back here without you."

She blushed and went away for his glass of lemonade. Curtis put the phone on the table where he could see it. A watched pot never boils, or was that a watchman with boils should never smoke pot? "This phone's not ringing," Curtis thought.

How weak could he be? "Let's see," he thought calling Demetria. She answered.

"It's uncanny how you call just before me every time," she said.

The line struck Curtis. Was this not a line? She had said the same thing last time and the time before.

"How are you?" she asked. "Thanks for giving me the option to explain the weekend. It really was a confusing time for me. I do want to let you know…"

Curtis cut her off. "You really don't have to explain," Curtis said.

"Okay, but I imagine you want to know what's going on with us, right?"

"That would be great. Help me understand what's really happening." Curtis was agitated with her stalling.

"I'm going to start by saying I really do love you, Curtis. I love everything about you. I love the way you make me feel when we are together. You are such a wonderful person, and I will always feel this way about you."

"Well, I'm glad you finally said it, Demetria. It seemed like it was hard for you to tell me how you felt."

"I am trying not to lose sight of the big picture, Curtis. Let me ask you this. If we decided that we would only be friends, what type of friendship would we have? Could we go out on double dates, or would that be a little over the top?"

"Double dates? What the hell?" thought Curtis.

"I'm having trouble coming to terms with our relationship, Curtis. It just doesn't sit well with me. I have been going to church with my daughter these past few weeks. I feel like I've finally awakened."

Curtis's stomach was sinking. She could have stopped there, but she continued. "I'm not going to say anything about my marriage. I do have to consider what's going on. I think I know you enough to say that we could have a wonderful life together, that you would make any woman a wonderful mate. I have learned so much from you. You make it so easy to be around you. You made it so easy for me to fall in love with you."

Curtis told himself he already knew all of this. This seemed to be the curtain for the real show. "Just say what you really want to say, Demetria."

"Okay. We, we have just met at the wrong time. I can't go through with it."

Curtis felt his eyes get misty. He sniffed and pulled the phone from his face, looked at it. He had not fallen for anyone like this since his first love. She had made him so lustful, the first one. This had to be Cupid's evil twin with the poisoned arrow working on his heart.

"What...I mean, what is it that you want?" Curtis asked her.

"I don't know. I just know that I can't keep you waiting."

He could have gone on his knees and begged. Curtis said instead, "Demetria, will I ever have a chance to be with you?"

"I can't say. I just don't know." Demetria hung up the phone.

Curtis had gotten back in his car, and the song on the radio was a familiar one. He had nothing to say. The song lyrics grew louder and louder in his head.

> Baby, please don't go
> Baby, please don't go
> Baby, please don't go
> Down to New Orleans
> You know I love you so
> Baby, please don't go

The more he sat, the more he couldn't rise. The more he thought of her, the more he had to try. He had to write and try and try to get this woman back who'd torn him so.

Dear Demetria,

I've read your text messages over and over. I read your e-mails over and over. I want to make sure I understand what you and they are saying.

What you've written is how I felt then and how I feel now. But you, you no longer feel what you once wrote? You will deny us now and smote the candle at a wick that is new and unused? How could you let something go that could turn out to be the best thing that's ever happened to you or to me? To us? You'd said one night that we do not know each other well enough. I think we know each other from lifetimes and lifetimes before. Everything has happened as if déjà vu with you my Demetria. We have been cut from the same cloth and through our travels have ended up exactly where we should be right now. I don't think that you and I being acquainted was an accident. It is fate. Fate, Demetria. You say that you have been going through a spiritual awakening. I can understand that because I asked that you come into my life, and I truly believe when you, Demetria, came, my prayers were answered. I have always been a spiritual person. I know that if you are sincere in what you ask for you will get whatever it is you ask for. If two people love each other, they shouldn't let anything get in the way. I asked you a long time ago when we were still at Dracoa if you were in love with your husband. If you had answered yes, I would not have pursued you. I only sought to win your heart, Demetria.

You sent this text a few months ago.

"I want to be with you. You are easy. I feel your spirit. I feel your soul. I like your heart. I trust you."

Demetria, if you feel this about someone, you go be with him. If it is for me, please don't cheat me out of the happiness you've already shown me wisps of. Don't let our life get away from us. We may never have this opportunity again.

Demetria never responded to Curtis's e-mail. That was his last effort. Only a stalker could keep trying after that. She always said the right things though she'd never said any more. Curtis was heartbroken. The only thing to do was get away. He didn't want to talk to anyone or see anyone. Curtis didn't leave his house for the weeks to come. He looked up relationships online and read about personality matches to try to understand. He still couldn't get Demetria off his mind. He had been through so much with her and had done things he had never done before. She seemed the perfect woman.

He had killed for her. God forbid he had killed that poor man for her. Had she ever loved him? Curtis pulled up several articles about relationship manipulations and one word appeared over and over. *Narcissist.*

I have learned Narcissist is usually very charming and pretty, and a delight on the surface and an uncanny knack of presenting themselves well to a target audience. They normally have the ability to make people feel very good and most will do anything to please her. They will continue to reward those who are doing for her as long as she needs you. Once her goals are accomplished and you are no longer useful, less time is spent on being charming and engaging.

A Typical Narcissist only cares about theirself. You are no more than the object that provides her with whatever it is she wants and needs: love, admiration, money, encouragement, support, etc.

The problem is that most men don't pick up on these things because their own high interest level blinds them to reality.

1. *She fails to exhibit any genuine curiosity about you, your life and what's important to you.* For example, while you are sharing about your passion for helping to save the whales, you can feel that she's preoccupied and just waiting for you to finish talking so she can tell you more about *her.*
2. *She keeps asking probing questions, attempting to determine how much money you make.* One of my students recently told me how his date, on their second night out together, asked him straight out: "So what's the most expensive gift you've ever given a woman?"

The bottom line is that this very beautiful, very charming (and extremely manipulative) young woman has absolutely no concern for others apart from those who are in a position to provide her with narcissistic supplies.

It occurred to Curtis that the article described Demetria. He would have never believed it if he had not read it with his own eyes. He realized that all the things he had gone through with her had been a waste of time. Still how his heart ached to realize he would never be with her. He had to give up loving her.

45

Curtis Goes Home

urtis went all the way back. He went back home to the old neighborhood where he had learned to throw a ball, to kiss a girl, to where he had grown up. Things had changed. The kids hanging on the block now were selling drugs instead of playing football. All the girls looked five times their age and were out trying to make a buck or two. Curtis saw where his old apartment was for rent. He had lived there briefly when he graduated high school. It was where he was living when he met Grace. Curtis rented it again. He had left all of his belongings. He moved in with just the clothes on his back. When he walked in overwhelmed with grief, aware fully now that everything in his life had crumbled around him, and he had come full circle. The apartment had not changed much since the last time he was there. A little new paint here and there was the only difference. Curtis was no longer the man he knew. He only wanted a lift now, something that would make him feel good. He bought a quarter sack of marijuana from a neighborhood kid on his bike. Curtis hadn't smoked since he graduated high school, but he wanted to smoke today.

Curtis thought the bag looked smaller than back in the day. "I guess inflation hits everyone," he said to the kid who grimaced and rode off. He took the bag home and in it was $20 worth of crack. This is not what he wanted. He had never tried crack. He had heard plenty of horror stories about this drug and was not planning on trying it. He scoured the dilapidated streets until he found the jit who had sold him the bag.

"Give me my money back. I wasn't buying crack," Curtis said.

"All sales final, old man," the jit said.

"Who in the fuck are you calling old?" Curtis said, stepping in to intimidate him. The jit reached into his hoodie pocket and pulled out his pistol.

"I'm calling you old, old man," he said. He smiled and revealed his gold caps.

"What in the hell am I supposed to do with this shit?"

"Listen, old man, you can eat that shit as far as I care, but you ain't getting a dime from me. I tell you what, mister. I know this little female who will tighten you up for that little piece of candy. I will send her your way," the jit said as he rode off on his bike, laughing.

Curtis looked around at the disheveled yards and houses. An old woman was sitting on her porch staring at him. She had seen hundreds of transactions from that porch over the years. Drug boys came and went. She thought that Curtis looked familiar, but it was far too long ago and what did it matter anyway. He headed back to his apartment.

Before Curtis could take a piss, a knock came on his door.

"Who is it?" Curtis asked.

"Dis Mustang," a female answered.

"Who?" Curtis said.

"Dis Mustang. Someone told me you had something for me."

Curtis remembered the jit's promise. "Hold on a minute," he said finishing up in the bathroom. Curtis finished pissing and went to the door. He pulled the crack out of his pocket to give to her. When he opened the door and saw a scantily dressed but still attractive young girl, he paused. She wore the streets upon her face and shoulders. It was sad to see her beauty wasted. He stood there silently gazing at her.

"Are you going to invite me in, mister?" Mustang asked. "Or are you gonna leave a girl out here all night?"

"I never asked you to come in the first place," Curtis thought.

Mustang, shrewd though she'd been beaten, realized the possibility of getting turned away. Her voice sweetened. "I was told that you might need a little company, and if not, that you had a package you didn't want."

Curtis held open his hand, extended it to her.

Her eyes lit up. "What a waste of her beauty," Curtis thought.

"Do you mind if I do it here, mister? I hate to walk around with this shit in my hand."

Why yes, he minded, of course, he minded, but pushed open the door and stepped by to let her in.

"It's a nice place you have here, mister. You live alone?" she asked.

"Why do you want to know?" he asked.

"Just asking." She sniffed at her bag and turned it in her hands longingly. "You never can tell. You might want me around with you. I might come knocking again," she said boldly.

"I don't think so," Curtis said.

Mustang retreated. "Just do what you have to do. I'd like to get some rest," Curtis said.

She was uncapping a ballpoint pen she'd pulled out from her handbag. The tip and ink were out from the pen. She had stuffed one end with some type of steel wool. "So this was how she'd smoke it," Curtis thought.

She took a small piece of the crack and placed it inside the steel wool, aimed a flame at the wool, and inhaled for thirty seconds. She exhaled and leaned back. Curtis noticed exhaling emitted no smoke. Mustang began to dance. She glided to the stereo, turned up the volume, returned to her pen, and took another hit. When it was out, she pinched off a little more from the bag, repacked the stem, and inhaled again.

"She's gone, boy she's gone," Curtis thought, both amused and disturbed. Mustang was beamed like a light out of storm clouds. She started undressing.

"I hope you don't mind," she said. She wore nothing under her hot pink dress.

"Knock yourself out," he said, rubbing his groin involuntarily. Something told him this was not supposed to be enjoyable, and yet, watching her had made him horny.

She licked her forefinger and stuck it in and out of her vagina. With her fingering herself while moaning to the music drowning out everything besides the scene, Curtis dropped his defenses. His anger melted into the sunlit room like days gone by. She was a crackhead, but she was turning him on. He took another sip of Grey Goose.

Mustang devoured the attention. Seeing Curtis rub himself, rise, and spread his legs to accommodate his rising provoked her. She put the stem down and pulled out a condom from her bag. She opened the condom and put it in her mouth as she walked toward Curtis. Curtis, erect, found it hard now to judge as he had once judged. Sex with prostitutes and crackheads was not much different from sex if it turned you on.

Mustang dropped to her knees, unzipped Curtis's pants, and pulled out his throbbing penis. She wrapped her lips delightfully around the shaft and inserted it inside the condom. Curtis had never seen anyone do this. There was some talent and practice involved in such an action. Mustang bobbed her head up and down on Curtis's penis. He laid back in his chair taken in and wanting to come. Before he could have his orgasm, Mustang rose, sat on his dick, and started riding him.

"You thought I was going to let you come alone?" she said, smiling, her eyes glazed and unknowable.

"I don't care what you do as long as you don't stop," he said.

Mustang became a frequent visitor. Curtis spent more money on her in a few weeks than all the chocolates and flowers he had ever bought. Not only was sex at his disposal, sex without strings, he had also adopted crack. Yes, crack was what'd never let him down. Crack even replaced the need for Mustang. He wanted the crack all to himself, and there was never enough. He had told Mustang on her last visit that he would call her whenever he wanted her to come by and do not just drop by anymore. With his smoking habit, he was going thru money as if it were water. And most times when he had gotten high, she didn't turn him on anymore. Curtis would have jumped over ten Mustangs for one hit of crack. She had become useless in his life. The only time he would call, would be to complain about the bullshit dope he had received and she would find another source, which she was compensated for.

He'd spend every day in search of the first hit. The first wonderful hit was like the first love, the first kiss, or the first breath, except that he would never get it. The first hit was an illusion that prevented him from doing anything else. He spent endless amounts of money to achieve one feeling, never to recapture it.

Luckily, Mustang came by to check on him since she had not heard from him in a while. It had been several months and she had been to rehab and cleaned her life up. She had actually grown attached to him and would come by every now and then to check on him. As she knocked on the door and waited patiently, she thought that she would try to convince him to let her stay the night. She had really missed the days and nights they had spent together, she wanted to show Curtis how she had gotten herself together and even convince him to do the same. She even had thoughts of settling down, if Curtis would have her. On the last trip to his house, she had slipped off the condom before Curtis inserted in penis into her without his knowledge. He had gotten so high he never realized that he was barebacked. She wanted to feel Curtis, and not the condom that had been present everytime before. She and Curtis had really gotten to know each other. On the nights they would get high, Curtis talked about all he had been through in the last few years. Mustang exposed her past to Curtis and he realized that their past wasn't much different. After waiting for a while, Curtis never answered. She knew he was there because he never left the house without the bike that he locked on the post on the front porch. She decided to go around a peek through the window, and to her astonishment, she seen Curtis's lifeless body lying on the floor. She ran around the back of the house, jimmied the back door open, and forced her way in. As she approached Curtis, she could see that he was still breathing but barely. She grabbed Curtis's phone and dialed 911 immediately. As she sat there waiting on the paramedics, she seen the crumpled up bag that Curtis had written his suicide not on. She realized that Curtis tried to take is own life. She didn't know that he was that unhappy, tears started to roll down her face. She had also come by to share some news with Curtis, but this would have to wait. She realized that she really had feelings for him.

46

Take a Bow

B eep…Beep…Beep…
Curtis awakened to the sounds of a hospital. He licked his lips and almost cut his tongue on them; they were so parched and chapped from the lack of food. He saw the tubes, needles, and pumps and monitors attached to him and all around. As he stirred, he loosened the finger clamp that connected his beating heart to the beeping vitals machine. That ascended to a monotonous quickened pace. A nurse appeared.

"So you decided to come back to life?" she asked.

Curtis had no answer. "I guess prayers help because you had a few people in here praying for you every night," she said. She reattached his pulse monitor. "The doctor will be glad that you're conscious. We didn't know how long you were going to be in a coma."

Curtis squinted and looked around him. The sun was peering through the window shades. He assumed it was very early morning. His eyes stopped at the cross on the nurse's gold chain. He vaguely recalled a dream of such a cross.

"Make sure you keep this on you finger from now on," she said. "We still have to keep a close eye on you."

"God is good," she said. The image of himself, a bottle of Grey Goose, exile, shouting, nightstand—all whirred in his head. He opened his mouth to speak. No sound came. He tried again.

"Were you here when I came in?" Curtis asked.

"Yes, I was the nurse on duty that day. Boy I tell you, you needed some rest." Curtis lowered his head in shame.

"You don't have to feel bad, Mr. Caldwell. I have seen far worse in my time."

"How long have I been here?" Curtis asked.

"Four months," the nursed answered. "You were in pretty bad shape when you got here. Your body had actually shut down. We didn't think you would make it."

Curtis lifted his hand and scratched his chin. They'd shaven him. His fingernails were cut, his hair combed. The nurse noticed Curtis looking at himself and smiled.

"Have you done all of this for me?" Curtis asked.

"No, darling, I'm just a nurse, not your stylist, but someone really cares about you. I don't think I could have done all she has done for you in the last two weeks."

Curtis looked over to the nightstand where there were fresh flowers, and a Bible. Curtis had forgotten about God in the past four or five years. When he and Grace were together, they had gone to church regularly. God had been a strong presence in their life. He remembered the pastor warning about the tenacity of the devil. He had said to Curtis, "You shall never let him enter into your home."

A chair sat in one corner next to the bright window. There was a purse sitting on the chair that he did not recgonize. Nothing looked familiar to Curtis. He felt tired.

"She has been here everyday since you got here," the nurse said. "She only leaves for work and when the doctor throws her out. She has made sure that we have done our job. I tell you, sometimes she was a little much, but we understood that she was here for the right reasons."

"It couldn't be Janice," he thought. Janice was married and moved. Anne had rekindled her relationship with her husband and was happy all over again. She had realized that Ty truly loved her and was committed to her. Her relationship with Curtis had actually helped her to return to her marriage and improve it. Devan—now Devan had vowed that she would never date another black man, remember? Curtis, apparently, had not been the only black man who'd promised her the world and fallen short or forgot to deliver. Demetria? No, he did not even want to utter the name. She never loved him. She took the insurance money and moved to South Florida with a guy almost half her age.

He was tired from thinking, from remembering. There was no one he could have expected this from. Curtis asked the nurse, "Who has been here?"

The nurse looked at him and said, "Why, you don't know?"

"No, I don't," Curtis answered.

"How could someone love you so much that she would sit her night and day, shave your face, and keep your fingernails cut, and you not know who it is? That woman has prayed for you every night and read the Bible with you. She has sacrificed two weeks when you were in the most critical stages of your coma to be by your side and probably would have been here for months if she had to."

Curtis felt like an ass. Nothing he had done in the past five years amounted to anything. It had been meaningless. He had not loved and had not been loved, and he had no idea who would care at this point. The nurse left him.

"You must count your blessings and understand more," she said. "Love is rare, and those who have it are there when you need them no matter what."

The phone rang as Curtis looked at his clean and limp fingers. "Hello," Curtis said.

"Dad, you're up!" Leigh said with excitement. "Oh, I love you so much. You scared the hell out of us."

"Hi, baby," Curtis said. "I'm sorry. I really screwed up, and I have been so selfish. I promise to be a different person and will never leave you unless it's really my time." The tears flowed down his face and soaked his hospital gown.

"I can't wait to pick Jr. up and tell him. We'll be there in a few minutes," she said.

"I'm not going anywhere," Curtis joked.

Before she could hang up, Curtis said, "Hey Leigh, have you been here at the hospital a lot?"

"Of course, Daddy, Junior and I come down there everyday."

"I have a question," Curtis said. "Who has been here with me all this time?"

Before Leigh could answer, Grace walked into the room.

Curtis looked at her and said, "Never mind," and placed the phone into its cradle.

"You're finally up?" Grace asked.

Curtis sobbed at the vision of his wife in front of him. "I am so sorry," he said over and over through his tears. "I am so sorry."

Grace came beside the bed, removed the phone from his lap and put her head against his chest. "I know," she said. "Everything is going to be all right—you'll see."

As Curtis and Grace lay there in bed together, someone was lurking in the shadows of the doorway. She never made her presence known, but she had an invested interest in Curtis. She had been there almost every day as well, and when Grace would go to work, she would come in and talk to Curtis while he laid there. She had told him that she had cleaned her life up and had a new lease on life, thanks to him. Their baby was now a little over a year, and she had brought him down to see Curtis every chance she could get. She named him with Curtis's middle name; he looked so much like his daddy.

www.ingramcontent.com/pod-product-compliance
Lightning Source LLC
Chambersburg PA
CBHW060233050426
42448CB00009B/1427